The Powe

How to Create a High-Performance Mind

John Newcombe and Michael Duff

MOMENTUM BOOKS

This edition published in 2012 by Momentum
Pan Macmillan Australia Pty Ltd
1 Market Street, Sydney 2000

A CIP record for this book is available at the National Library of
Australia

The Power Within: How to Create a High-Performance Mind

EPUB format: 9781743340615
Mobi format: 9781743340622
Print on Demand format: 9781743340639

Cover design by XOU Creative
Copyedited by Mark Evans
Proofread by Hayley Crandell

Macmillan Digital Australia: www.macmillandigital.com.au

To report a typographical error, please email
errors@momentumbooks.com.au

Visit www.momentumbooks.com.au to read more about all our books
and to buy books online. You will also find features, author interviews
and news of any author events.

Table of Contents

Just because the road ahead is long is no reason to slow down.

Just because there is much work to be done is no reason to get discouraged.

It is a reason to get started, to grow, to find new ways, to reach within yourself and discover strength, commitment, determination, discipline.

The road ahead is long and difficult, and filled with opportunity at every turn.

Start what needs starting.

Finish what needs finishing.

Get on the road. Stay on the road. Get on with the work.

Right now you're at the beginning of the journey.

What a great place to be! Just imagine all the things you'll learn, all the people you'll meet, all the experiences you'll have.

Be thankful that the road is long and challenging, because that is where you'll find the best that life has to offer.
— Ralph Marston

Introduction

John Newcombe

It was 26 December 1953, and I sat by the radio in the living room of our Sydney home listening to day one of the Davis Cup finals between Australia and the United States. After four days (due to some rain delays on day three), Australia won 3–2.

Two 19- year-olds were representing Australia in that match and they went on to become two of the greatest world champions. Their names were Lew Hoad and Ken Rosewall. I was nine-and-a-half years old and, like thousands of kids around the country, I dreamed of playing tennis for Australia one day.

Ten years later my dream became a reality when I played my first Davis Cup match for Australia. Thirteen years later, in 1967, I reached my first Wimbledon final and won the title; sixteen years later, in 1970, I walked onto the Centre Court at Wimbledon to do battle with Ken Rosewall in the final. In 1969, in between those two finals, I suffered my only loss in a Wimbledon final out of ten attempts (singles and doubles) to the legend Rod Laver. Following my victory over Ken in 1970, I successfully defended the title in 1971. By the time I had retired, I had also added six

Wimbledon doubles titles, two Australian Open titles, two US Opens and eleven other Grand Slam doubles titles – 24 Grand Slam titles in all.

Twenty years after that dream as a young kid, I had not only made it to the top of the tennis mountain, I had achieved much more than I had dreamed of.

So what was it that got me to the top? Was I born with certain qualities? Was it the great advice or coaching I had along the way? Was it the positive role that my parents played, or was I just a natural self-starter?

The answer is all of these things and a few more. Getting to the top of any profession doesn't just happen, it takes a lot of hard work and constant learning. The saying that you learn more from your losses than your wins was one that I found carried a lot of truth.

I have always been fascinated with the subject of men and women being able to achieve their maximum potential. For some it has appeared to be a relatively straightforward journey; for most it is a more prolonged journey as they gradually put together the pieces that make up the final puzzle.

I have thought about writing this type of book for some time and in order to make the book a more complete work I asked my good friend Michael Duff to add his thoughts and ideas to my experiences.

Mike spent twenty years as an executive in the business world, ten of them leading international sporting bodies in golf and tennis. For the past ten years he has been running his own business as a very successful corporate professional mentor.

I believe our combined approach and insights to the world of elite performance are applicable to any pursuit and will be of great benefit to anybody wanting to succeed and get the best from life.

Michael Duff

For most of my early corporate life it never occurred to me that I could learn how to create success for myself. In fact I had never really taken the time to stop and think about how to create success. I suppose I considered it all a random game of chance and that if the 'planets all aligned' I might make it. I had never stopped to think about what it took to be successful and I certainly did not know that I could train myself to think differently and create an easier path to success for myself. I took for granted that corporate life was challenging and difficult most of the time and that stress and anxiety went with the territory. I assumed that those who made it to the top were somehow genetically different, or just lucky.

At the relatively young age of 28 I was headhunted to the role of CEO of the Australasian PGA Tour, the men's pro golf circuit. After five very challenging years at the helm, I was offered a senior leadership role with the ATP Tour, the global men's pro tennis circuit. I was responsible for a territory that covered approximately half the globe, I travelled 26 weeks of the year and there was an enormous amount of information and politics for me to stay on top of. While I loved the glamour of the role and the many exciting places I got to visit and do business in, it was nonetheless a stressful role. Or at least that's how it was for me.

During my time out from the business of sport I got

the chance to relax sitting courtside watching the best players in the world do battle. It didn't take long for me to work out how important mental strength was in determining who would finish on top. A great array of shots from all parts of the court wasn't enough. An ability to think clearly under pressure and to stay strong and positive when they were struggling was what defined the great champions.

It occurred to me that even though I had risen to very senior roles in my career I was a complete novice when it came to building a strong mind. When confronted with a challenge, I was more likely to find myself anxious and stressed than calm, determined and clear.

In 1998, I resolved that it was time for me to 'go back to school' and to build up the strength of my mind. With some of the most successful people in their chosen fields as my mentors, I found that while there is always something new to learn the foundations are quite simple and even a small gain can produce amazing results.

I was fortunate that I had the chance to learn from the best in the world, including my close friend John Newcombe. On many occasions I would use Newk as a sounding board, exploring a particular insight and how I might put it into practice for myself.

Often Newk would respond to my newly learnt insight with a nod of understanding and then explain his perspective on the subject. Early on in our friendship, it became clear to me that one of Newk's greatest strengths was this understanding of his own mind and his ability to create a strong mental perspective. Whether winning Wimbledon or an Australian Open title, the side bet with mates on the golf course, or in his business dealings, Newk has built a life around achieving the outcomes he has set out to achieve.

Imagine for a moment how it would be if that was what your life was like – one where you consistently achieved what you wanted to achieve. Importantly, as I have observed Newk at close quarters over the past 20 years or so, I have been impressed by his calm, thoughtful and determined approach. Regardless of what is going on around him, he remains calm and mentally in control.

Many books have been written on the subject of understanding and creating success in life; our aim is for this book not to be another one of them that simply gathers dust on the shelf. When I started the journey for myself in the mid-1990s, I was after a very practical approach. I was more interested in the practices used by the best than I was in the theories expressed by those who had still to achieve their own success.

As I have learned the concepts in this book, I have personally applied them to my own life and experimented and fine-tuned my approach. I know from experience that they work. I was also after a simple approach. Too often I found the approaches of others overly complex and difficult to follow.

The life I lead today is one that I did not believe was possible for me. I might from time to time have dreamt of living like this but it was only ever a dream. That is, until I started this journey.

For the past ten years I have been sharing what I learnt from Newk and others with corporate leaders and their teams through the MINDsense program.

It is a blessing and a great joy to be constantly in demand to share this knowledge. The changes that people have made in their lives as a result of applying the MINDsense approach are many and varied and are in themselves a fantastic reward for me. Losing weight, quitting smoking, improving relationships, earning promotions or greater incomes are just a few of them.

If you have the will, this book will provide the skill.

It is indeed an honour and a privilege to collaborate with Newk in bringing this book to you.

Chapter 1

Who is John Newcombe?

Mike

If we're going to explore some of Newk's insights to performing at your best it would probably be useful to first explore who John Newcombe is.

I don't mean in a physical sense, his height, weight or physique. I also don't mean in the sense of what it is he does, being a tennis player, husband, father and businessman. I also don't mean what it is he has in terms of assets and wealth. What I mean is: when you strip all that away, who is the man behind the man? What is at the inner core of John Newcombe?

When I think of Newk, I think of a guy who is handsome, athletic, charismatic, talented and determined. If I go a bit deeper I could add tenacious, resilient, successful, strong, disciplined, generous and focused. I could go on.

Over the years as I have come to know Newk, I have seen many sides to this very successful man. We have experienced triumphs together and we have witnessed tragedy together. What really matters though is not who I think Newk is but who Newk thinks he is. When Newk contemplates his very existence, what words would he use to describe who he is? Who does he see himself as?

Over time I have come to understand that the most important influencing aspect of our life lies simply in our sense of ourselves – who we think we are; who we see ourselves as. If I think of all the truly successful people I have had the pleasure to meet, the single common factor is a strong sense of self, without limitation.

By truly successful I mean people who live in harmony with their world, consistently achieving the outcomes they desire and predominantly spending life with a smile on their face and a laugh in their voice – people who are happily achieving in life and who possess both the strength of mind and the complete belief in their ability to deal with whatever challenges life throws at them.

Now contemplate this for yourself. Who are you? Describe yourself. What words would you use to define your sense of yourself?

I'll let Newk answer for himself in his response, but I have no doubt that his sense of himself will be a strong, positive one. I came to realise on my own journey, as many others have before me, that how you see yourself is the self-fulfilling prophecy that determines completely how you experience life.

Over the course of our childhood and adolescent years, we start to associate with our inner sense of self. This is not so much a conscious, considered and thoughtful process but rather a subconscious process where the mind takes over the process in an autopilot sort of way for us. We don't consciously construct this sense of ourselves; our mind does it for us as we experience life.

A view starts to form in our subconscious mind of who we think we are. This view, this perception we have of ourselves, becomes so real that we use phrases like 'That's my personality' as if it is a hard-wired, fixed state of being. The challenge, though, is that it is an illusion – an illusion that often becomes a prison cell. How we ultimately come to see ourselves is determined to a large extent by the events of our lives and how these events shape the view we have of ourselves, most of which is happening subconsciously. Different life experiences create different perceptions of self, which we will explore in later chapters.

Within our sense of self, there are both positive and negative perceptions– areas where we believe in ourselves and others where we are less certain and have insecurities and self-doubts. The positive elements in our sense of self serve us well, as they are ultimately an expression of our own self-belief. When we believe, we are empowered. When faced with opportunities or challenges we 'can' and 'do'. The negative elements, however, shape us in a much more limiting way as an inner expression of disbelief or doubt. When we don't believe, our path is blocked and we often feel powerless to get past the block.

Either way, the positive or negative perspectives that we have of ourselves are simply and mostly a consequence of someone else's point of view. Positive reinforcement, encouragement or praise as a child led us to form a positive view of ourselves, whilst criticism or the expression of doubt by others led to our negative views. Ultimately, your true inner sense of self was not created by you; it was not of your conscious choosing. Your environment, circumstances and the people around you in your childhood years all contribute to the formation of your view of yourself. Some people get lucky and spend their childhood in a positive, nurturing environment; unfortunately, some don't.

I know this from personal experience. Throughout the first 20 years of my life my sense of self was evolving. This is true for all of us. As a consequence of a very supportive, encouraging and nurturing family home, my sense of self was quite strong when I set out into the big wide world as an adult, but there were a few fears lurking beneath the surface that held me back. At a subconscious level, I associated with a mind-held view that I was supposed to be a successful human being, someone who achieved and did well in life. Lots of positive reinforcement and praise as a child led me to contemplate that there were expectations about who I would turn out to be. During this time I had been unaware of what was going on in my subconscious mind, as it created a sense of self that had a strong association with success. Now my mind sought to ensure that I live up to that expectation. Fears – like failure, what other people thought of me, or not living up to others' expectations – soon turned up all too often in my thinking and with those fears came stress.

Thankfully, in my late thirties my eyes were opened to the importance of having a strong sense of myself and letting go of the limiting associations I had allowed to form in my mind – letting go of my insecurities and self-doubt by seeing them as the illusions that they were. I started to work through those fears. I spent time exploring who I was and how I had become that person. I sought to understand why I responded to life the way I did and what triggered the various emotions I felt. I ultimately got myself to a place where I had a much, much stronger sense of myself and most importantly a sense of self that I had chosen rather than the one created randomly by the events of my life. Then my life changed.

I learnt from people like Newk and others the importance of analysing my thoughts, of learning to think about *how* I was thinking and training myself to think differently.

You would think that over the thousands of years of human evolution we would have worked out how to improve this fundamentally important aspect of our existence, but we haven't, and there is a very simple reason why.

Well, it's a very simple reason when you understand it; the problem is that at a certain level your mind will resist learning this. When you understand why your mind does this, though, you find the key that unlocks true happiness and the realisation of your potential. I know that sounds like a big statement, but I have found this fundamental understanding present in every human being I have met who is living at a higher level.

You need to make sense of your mind. You need to understand how it works – not in a complex neurological sense but in a day-to-day 'how I experience life' sense. We hope to make that discovery simpler and easier for you.

Newk's response

It is a very interesting and challenging question Mike has asked me. Who is John Newcombe?

There's no simple answer. I'd like to think I'm a bit

more than simple, but it isn't really all that complex either. I feel I have evolved as a person every ten years of my life, so today I am not the same person as I was in my forties.

I look around me and often see people who seem resigned to who they are. 'That's just who I am', they might say. I know that as my life has changed and my goals and aspirations have shifted through the journey of my life I have needed to constantly evolve. To achieve each of these goals I couldn't just stay as I was. I needed to grow. My view of who I am capable of being and what I am capable of achieving has been a constant work in progress. Perhaps I'm fortunate to have a strong enough belief in myself that I can constantly change, but I think this is something we can all learn and in fact we need to learn if we are to really enjoy life and experience it to the max.

There was nothing really outstanding I can remember about my first ten years. Our family life was reasonably stable. My dad was a dentist, my mum was a mother and housewife and my relationship with my elder and younger sisters was without serious incident, except for the occasional 'blue' when I tried to get out of the washing up after dinner, pleading with Dad that it was a girls' job.

From the age of ten until I was 40 I was on a constant roll of achievement in the various areas that I'd set my mind on. My life dream began at nine and a half as I listened to that Davis Cup final and decided that one day I would play Wimbledon and represent Australia in Davis Cup.

I think it is important to note here that my goal

was not so much to win Wimbledon as it was to compete there.

I wanted to play Wimbledon and Davis Cup and to experience the excitement that I had felt as I listened to those great matches as a boy. I wanted to experience the atmosphere and the history and tradition and to feel the thrill of representing my country. I didn't need to win, though. I didn't see winning as a necessity, a sort of validation of myself. I always thought I was fundamentally OK, and the experience would be a wonderful addition to my life.

One of my favourite sayings is: 'Never be afraid to dream and to follow your dreams, but never allow the dream to become your master.'

My interpretation of that is always to be looking ahead and planning your road to the future, but the reality check is where you are in the present. Life is ahead of us, not behind us, so only go to the past to learn from your experiences, ensuring that negative actions are not repeated and that positive actions are built upon and practised.

As we work our way through this book, I will build on these themes by analysing some of my own real-life experiences from challenging circumstances, some of which were extreme pressure situations.

The teen years were the ones where I was defining myself and my character. Early on in my tennis career I realised that to win matches I needed to understand the weaknesses and strengths in my 'natural' character. I was constantly challenging myself around what I believed I was capable of as I sought to become as strong as possible. In a way, but without consciously realising it at the time, I suppose I was doing what Mike alluded to earlier – deciding who I was going to be.

My strengths and weaknesses at the time displayed themselves off the court as well as on the court in the heat of battle. By the time I was 20, I had a pretty good idea of the areas I needed to work on in order to try and perfect my mental strength and character under pressure. Of course simply being aware of the issues is one thing; putting it into practice in real situations until you are confident of your ability to control any attempt by the negative forces to enter the body and mind is the real test. By negative forces I am referring to those associated with self-doubt – the negative forces that at times had me questioning my ability or strength, that led to fear or anxiety and interrupted the flow of energy I needed to be able to play at my best.

The strongest message I send to kids playing tennis today is this: 'The greatest enemy and opponent you will ever face is the Negative Force. This force is real and it will try and enter your body at any time that you are challenging yourself. It is important for you to recognise and acknowledge this force, for only by doing that can you learn how to beat it!'

The key lesson for me was that my greatest opponent was not on the other side of the net – it was on my side. More specifically it was in my head and in my thoughts. It was an opponent only I could conquer, but in order to conquer it I first needed to understand it.

As we progress through the book, I'll relate some encounters of this battle and how it was won.

Once the Negative Force has entered your body, it

turns into what we know as fear, which in turn numbs your mind, body and general reactions. Driving these forces out of your body takes a very practised and experienced mind. I have had the occasion to do this under the extreme pressure conditions of a Wimbledon singles final. I was just as proud of this achievement in overcoming the Negative Force as I was of capturing this great world event.

By my thirties I had completed my tennis career at the top of the mountain and spent the next decade building on the business interests I had started the previous decade while I was still playing. I commenced the earliest of these commercial associations at 23 years of age, as I'd observed many athletes ending their sporting careers at 30 and then not knowing what to do with themselves. I chose not to leave things to chance and to become much more the master of my own destiny.

This goes back to my earlier point of living in the present, learning from the past and planning for the future.

My forties were spent in an entirely different manner as I got involved in community and charity work. It became more about what I could put back in than what I took out. Two of the more important roles for me were with the National Australia Day Council [NADC] and the Starlight Foundation. The NADC is a federal body appointed by the Government to promote Australia Day, 26 January, each year. I was asked to chair this council, which I did for ten years. One of our jobs was to select the Australian of the Year, which I always found fascinating as we read through the dossiers on a hundred or more Aussies who had achieved great things, many of them in a quiet way.

The Starlight Foundation's primary role is to grant wishes to kids who are chronically or terminally ill. I was a founding board member of this charity and stayed in that position for 11 years. This experience was both extremely rewarding and also humbling, in seeing how the kids and their families handled adversity – the strength and resolve they showed as they dealt with such sadness and tragedy.

In my fifties I reverted again to personal achievement as Tony Roche and I took over the captain/coach role of the Australian Davis Cup team. This was a great seven years with my very close mate and long-time doubles partner as we helped a talented group of young men go through the trials and tribulations of developing and maximising their talents. Five years later, Australia had become the best team in the world. Tony and I found this experience to be immensely rewarding.

The Japanese have a huge celebration when a person turns 70, as they see this as when he/she has reached the age of wisdom. As I'm in my mid-sixties at the time of writing this, the one thing I do know is that I know a heck of a lot more now than I did in my twenties!

I'm excited about doing this book with Mike. I believe that by combining our thoughts and experiences and expressing them in different ways, we will create some breakthrough material which may help some people have a better understanding of themselves, thereby living a more enjoyable, successful life with family, friends and business acquaintances.

Mike's observations

It's so clear for me that at the core of John's successes in life is his high level of self-belief. He had the strength as a teenager to be able to explore the areas where he knew he needed to develop, to face his own weaknesses and demons and not to shy away, not be overcome by fear as he pursued his dreams, and finally to be able to step into greatness. Think about who John needed to think he was in order to be able to do that, how strong his sense of self was.

As he mentions, his upbringing wasn't particularly remarkable. Perhaps it was a combination of his imagination as he thought about the excitement of one day being on Centre Court at Wimbledon, along with his realisation that he needed to understand himself and how his mind and body worked and then strengthen them, which laid the foundation for his remarkable career.

Imagine being able to look at your opportunities in life and to express to yourself the view that you can mix it with the best – to stay focused on that goal and to resist the opinions of others as they express their own limiting self-beliefs and try to project them onto you; and to do that over and over through the course of your life.

So often in my role of mentoring corporate executives as we explore their goals and aspirations and I push them beyond playing a 'safe game', they express a whole swag of reasons why it wouldn't be possible for them. Imagine what people might have said to Newk when he said he wanted to play Davis Cup or at Wimbledon. He was free to explore these opportunities, without any guarantees, because his self-belief supported him in having a go. In life there are no guarantees but I know, and you know, you can't achieve anything without first trying, without first having a go.

In my journey, I taught myself a process that I've followed for the past decade so that what I do today and what I take on in life is way beyond what I thought was possible for me. I no longer need to play a 'safe game' and life is way more rewarding and exciting.

I think a critical element in John's response was that his goal was not so much to win as to compete at Wimbledon. As a consequence, I believe he became very focused on continually improving his game to get it to the level required to play at the highest level. It was not so much a focus on winning but focusing on what was required to enable him to participate. I have repeatedly found that this is the hallmark of all great champions who are able to sustain results at the highest level – those who have an enduring career at the pinnacle of their profession.

This ties in with John's comments about 'living in the present and learning from the past'. As he developed his game, he used the past as a reference point to identify areas for improvement and then focused on the present moment and on the improvement of the identified area through the actions he was engaged in at that moment. He spent hours and hours on the practice court developing and honing his game. How much time do you spend practising and developing your skills? Time on the practice court is time spent role-playing, putting yourself into situations you will experience in life and practising your response. Most corporate people I deal with spend little time practising or role-playing, yet they expect improvement.

You don't win Wimbledon by being completely focused on *winning* it in an isolated sense. The player who performs the best for the two weeks will come away with the title. The player who deals with all that is thrown at them over the fortnight and whose game and physical and mental strength is in the best shape wins the crown – one match at a time!

To arrive ready to have your best chance, you need to work on improving all aspects of your game and your physical and mental abilities. If you do that better than anybody else, you give yourself the best chance of winning. If you place too much focus on the result or on the title, the chances are that you will choke under the self-imposed pressure.

Imagine if you focused solely on improving your ability, your skill or your strength of mind and that you were able to improve by one per cent every day. Where would you be in 100 days? Twice as good as you are now. Now imagine what results you would get in your work if you were twice as good as you are now.

Chapter 2

The MINDsense Model

Mike

I'm a firm believer in keeping things simple. As I was piecing together the different things I was learning from the world's best, I looked for a way to tie all the elements together. I came to understand the connection between the outcomes I sought to achieve and my actions. Without action, without having a go, there would be no outcomes. I also came to appreciate the impact that my feelings or emotions had on my ability to take action and, finally, how all of this was underpinned by my beliefs.

From this understanding I was able to develop a simple model that linked each of these aspects of the human condition to each other. Perhaps most importantly, though, this model provided a navigational aid that helped me to get what I wanted in the most efficient, effective and peaceful manner. It changed my life!

Think about that for a moment. If you set out on a journey to a distant destination by car, you wouldn't leave unless you knew the route. If you had no prior experience in navigating your way to this place, you would carry with you a map or a satellite navigation device to ensure you reached the destination in the most direct and efficient way. It is very rare in life that when we go on a road trip we don't reach our destination. We trust the method of navigation we use and the processes we use along the way. If you just pulled out of your driveway without any idea of where your destination was, you would no doubt take lots of wrong turns and although you might ultimately, through trial and error, reach your destination, it would be a far from efficient process.

In life there are lots of destinations you will attempt to reach, goals you will seek to achieve and outcomes you will desire. Do you have a navigational process which you use to make sure you always get to where you want to go and achieve what you want to achieve? Or is the journey one of chance, one of hit and miss? Are you relying on luck? What if life was like most of your road trips where you always reach the desired outcome because you have a navigational system or process that consistently works and that you trust?

As you reflect on your life today, is it littered with missed opportunities and failed journeys? Perhaps you have even become resigned to the view that you can't get to where you want to go, you can't achieve what you want from life. This would be based on your past experiences. You may even have convinced yourself that your earlier expectations were unrealistic and have since abandoned them. And you have probably found lots of proof to support the notion that your expectations were 'unrealistic'. If this is your life, there is hope if you learn to understand why this happens.

Imagine for a moment what it would be like if you had a compass that helped you navigate life, which ensured you always got to your destination or achieved your desired goal. Have you ever stopped to wonder why some people always seem to get what they want out of life? Why do some people have the lives that they want? Perhaps your mind simply put it down to good luck or even some fortunate genetic disposition. I know mine did.

The model you are about to be introduced to is such a navigational tool. It has been working for me for the past ten years and I have complete belief in the power of applying it. I didn't create it, though. It has been in play for centuries, often as an unconscious process employed by successful people. When I have explained it to world champions, they have often confirmed their understanding and application of a similar process, without consciously putting a framework to it.

At a certain point in my own journey into this area, I simply decided one day that if this approach, or a derivation of it, was good enough for the best in the world then surely it was good enough for me. I surrendered to it and got out of my own way!

I call it the MINDsense model and it has become the foundation to the way I live and to what I teach the corporate executives I mentor.

Let me explain.

Let's call your life as it is today the result. The model will help you understand how you got to this point in life, although it can also be used to help you to achieve any particular result that you desire in life – individual goals like buying a new car or house, losing weight or gaining a promotion.

Let's use it to understand your life. To best understand how it works, it is useful to work through the model backwards.

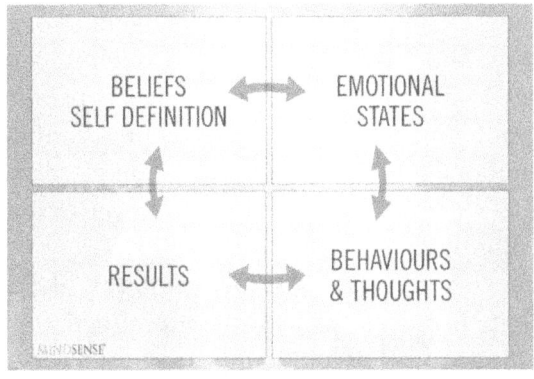

This life that you have, this result, is a consequence of your behaviours and your thoughts. All of the actions you have taken and all of the thoughts you have had throughout the course of your life have created the life that you experience today. The way in which you have responded to the events of your life and your opportunities through your actions and your thoughts have determined what life looks like for you.

Put another way, you have gone through your life in a state of constant thought and action and the end result of all of those thoughts and actions is your life as it is today.

How we act and think is in turn influenced by our emotional state, how we are feeling at any point in time. The actions that we take will be influenced by our emotional state, as will the way in which we think about things. In the following examples you will see that behaviours and thoughts are a consequence of different emotions.

If we are feeling curious we will seek to understand by asking questions and listening. The emotion of feeling curious leads to the behaviour of asking questions and listening. If we are feeling angry or frustrated, we may raise our voice, express disappointment or argue. If we are feeling confident or certain about something, we will be decisive and take action. If we are feeling anxious or uncertain, we will act hesitantly or not act at all.

As a general rule, positive emotions like feeling confident, focused, curious or determined support a wider range of behaviours and therefore more actions are available to us. Positive emotions are empowering. These positive emotions not only support us taking action, they also help us to think clearly. Our thoughts are more positive and empowering.

Counter to that, if we are feeling stressed, anxious, frustrated or resigned, we will be less inclined to take appropriate action and may even find ourselves somewhat paralysed. These negative emotions limit effective action and tend to shut down access to clear thinking. How well do you think when you are intensely angry?

When you are feeling 'on top of the world', there's not much you can't do; when you are feeling depressed, there's not much you can do.

Stop for a moment and reflect on this. When you were feeling positive, what sort of action did you take, how did you think? You will no doubt recall that you were in a more empowered state at this time.

As you look around yourself in life, you will witness all sorts of people experiencing all sorts of emotions throughout each day. You will no doubt experience your own emotional roller-coaster at times. Have you ever stopped to contemplate why we feel the emotions that we do? If you are like most people, you probably just take them for granted and may even have developed a habit of blaming other people or circumstances for these emotions. Perhaps, as we will explore, the actions of others or the events of our lives aren't the real culprits, though. Perhaps the answers are much closer to home.

What influences how you feel in life, the emotions that you experience from one moment to the next, are the beliefs that you have about yourself and the sense that you have about who it is that you are – your self-definition. That mental association *your subconscious mind* has created, based on your circumstances and life experiences, about who it is you have come to think you are is the perspective that *you* have of who it is that you think you are. This self-definition that you have is often described as your comfort zone.

It is how that self-definition – that sense of self – fits with your environment or circumstances from moment to moment in life which determines how you will feel. Take a moment now to contemplate that last statement. Understanding this simple principle is incredibly empowering.

Let's explore further.

Listen to how you describe yourself, the words you use to explain who you are. By this, I mean think about how many ways you can finish the sentence that begins with 'I am'. There are literally hundreds of ways. Consider how it is that you see yourself. Are you strong or weak, determined or easily distracted, tenacious or quick to throw in the towel, good at maths or no good at maths, quick to get angry or relatively calm and peaceful, capable of solving your challenges or often overwhelmed by them?

Who do you think you are? How did you come to have this view of yourself? Perhaps the events of your life were the most significant contributor to this view rather than it being some genetic predisposition.

If you are somewhat depressed by how your life is unfolding, if you are feeling overwhelmed by your circumstances, what sits at the core of your depressed or overwhelmed state? Using our model, the answer to your emotional state can be found in your beliefs and self-definition. Behind these depressing and overwhelming feelings lies the belief that you can't solve the issue you have, that it is all too hard. These beliefs are supported by a sense of self that is probably articulated as: 'I'm just not strong enough, I don't know what to do and I can't find the energy to try.'

Does this sense of self along with those beliefs support overcoming the obstacles that life has presented to us? Absolutely not. Consider the alternative, though: the belief that there is no challenge in life I can't find a solution to; the sense I have of myself is that I am strong, capable, determined and tenacious.

The great opportunity in life lies in how we develop our beliefs and sense of self, whether we seek to consciously and continuously improve and develop it or whether we become resigned to what it is and therefore who we are.

As we will explore, your subconscious mind would prefer that you didn't expand your beliefs and sense of self. It would prefer that you maintain your existing beliefs and self-view so that you remain constant and predictable. We go through life justifying our sense of self by describing it as our 'personality'. What we don't realise is that this personality of ours becomes a life sentence which we constantly reinforce and validate, but ultimately get stuck with.

Even as you read through this, you will probably find yourself resisting this concept. 'No, it's not true. I really can't fix this. I'm not really that strong or capable.'

Let's explore this sense of self, particularly those views we have of ourselves that create or reinforce limitations or negative beliefs. Let's explore how many ways we could complete the sentence that begins with 'I am':

'I am shy.'

'I am not very good in new crowds.'

'I am no good at maths.'

'I am a night owl.'

'I am no good unless I get nine hours sleep.'

'I am no good at tolerating slow drivers.'

These are all like a set of instructions to the mind. This describes who you are, or at least who you think you are. It all seems very real, but as we will explore later it isn't. Whoever you see yourself as is the self-fulfilling prophecy that determines how your life unfolds, completely.

Let's consider this concept from a different perspective. Think about shyness. Where does shyness come from, where does it reside in the human body? You will recognise that it resides in your mind, wherever that is, and your mind is accessed through thought. Perhaps shyness resides simply in thought. Now, most people who are shy will probably want you to believe that it is genetic, a sort of life sentence that they are stuck with. They will point to their parents who were shy or their brothers and sisters who are shy as proof of their gene pool. Maybe it was simply their association with shy people which helped them to subconsciously form the view in their own minds that they were also shy. If this is you, notice how strongly your mind is fighting the view that I just expressed, how it is defending your shyness. We'll explore this defence mechanism in a later chapter.

We know that humans are capable of conscious thoughts, of being able to consciously stop and control the thoughts we have. Therefore we are ultimately able to control our thoughts and, if shyness is accessed through our thoughts, then we have the ability to control it. Notice how we allow ourselves to think it is so real and unchangeable – an immovable 'personality trait'.

Now consider the concept of the human personality. Again, we hear it so often expressed as a fixed, immovable state of being, almost as if it is entirely hard-wired into us as part of our genetic make-up. Contemplate for a moment where it is that your personality resides in your physiology. Again, you will recognise that it resides in your mind as the expression of your sense of self. It is the expression of who you have come to see yourself as.

As Descartes so eloquently put it, 'I think, therefore I am.' If I think I am shy, I will be shy. We have all learnt to believe things about ourselves and we develop such a strong attachment to these beliefs that they become completely real to us. They just are. We don't challenge them. In fact, we seek to prove that these beliefs are true, a sort of self-validation of who it is that we think we are.

By the time you are in your mid to late twenties, think about how many ways you could finish this sentence: 'I am . . .'

Some of the sentences you complete will focus on your strengths, the very things that create possibilities and empower you. However, some will focus on perceived limitations and weaknesses and then shut down opportunities and possibilities because they don't support them.

This sense of self also plays a significant role in determining the emotions you feel each day. That's right, your self-definition is responsible. Yet you, like most people, have probably become accustomed to handing over that responsibility for your emotions to other people or things:

'Jack made me so angry.'

'I am so frustrated, he's late again with the report.'

'He always makes me feel anxious.'

'Sue always makes me happy.'

'I always feel great when Terry is around.'

Let's go back to the MINDsense model again. What influences your emotional state are your beliefs about yourself and your sense of yourself. To help understand this, let's first explore positive emotions followed by negative emotions.

Positive

When what it is that you believe about yourself supports the situation you find yourself in, you will experience positive emotions and feel good. If I believe in my ability to accomplish a task, I will feel confident. If my sense of myself is that I am strong and capable, then in a new social situation I will be calm and confident and possibly excited. If nothing in your environment is threatening your sense of yourself, you will feel good. Expressed another way, if you believe in your ability to deal with the circumstances you find yourself in, all will be good in your world. Your sense of yourself, your beliefs about yourself and your world, are in harmony.

In other words, you are in your comfort zone. Your environment is not challenging or threatening that comfort zone, your sense of self.

Negative

Now, consider for a moment the opposite of this: when I challenge you and your comfort zone, when I push the boundaries of what it is that you believe about yourself, when who it is that you see yourself as doesn't completely support the circumstances that you find yourself in. This is when we feel those negative emotions like anxiety, stress, or feeling overwhelmed.

If I am expected to undertake a task that I don't believe I can achieve, I will find myself feeling anxious. If I am unsure of myself, then the first few minutes after I walk into a party will be stressful and awkward.

We will explore the other significant negative emotions of frustration and anger a little later, as their causes are slightly different and warrant further discussion.

Perhaps like many you just thought that the emotions you felt were part of some random act of life, a cruel act from a higher being that in a twisted moment decided today was just not your 'lucky day'.

Let me give you a couple of examples.

Let's say you believe you are good at maths and you would describe yourself to others as being good at maths. Through school you did well in maths and when confronted with most mathematical challenges you can work them out. This belief most likely came about as a result of people expressing their belief in you, praising you for your application at school and encouraging you to be even better.

If I give you a maths problem to solve which you believe you can solve, you will find yourself feeling confident. This confidence will lead to you taking the necessary action to solve the maths problem, which will in turn reinforce the underlying notion that you have of yourself: 'I'm pretty good at maths.' Beliefs impact emotions that support behaviours and ultimately produce a result.

What if you don't believe you're any good at maths? The maths problem I give you may be outside your comfort zone, in other words outside what you believe about yourself. You may then find yourself feeling either anxious or resigned about solving it. If you feel anxiety, this will interrupt your access to clear thinking and you will possibly become even more stressed until at some point you throw in the towel with added resignation: 'I knew I was no good at maths.' Again, beliefs impact emotions and behaviours, only this time in a limiting or negative sense.

You may find yourself somewhere in between, where you believe you are OK at maths, but not great.

With enough belief, you will take on solving the maths problem but you may not feel particularly confident as you do.

Let's consider public speaking. If, for whatever reason, be it years of practice or lots of training, you believe you are capable of addressing an audience, you will find yourself confident in taking on this challenge. You may have a little apprehension but not enough to stop you. If you contemplate your sense of self at this point, you will see yourself as 'someone who just does these things', 'someone who can'.

The positive emotion of feeling confident supports you doing the things necessary to perform, such as making the necessary preparations and ultimately getting up in front of the audience.

Your self-belief, your sense of yourself, supports the circumstances you find yourself in, you feel confident and you take appropriate action.

On the flip side, let's look at what happens if you do not believe in your ability to speak publicly. As we will explore, these beliefs are a consequence of conditioning in life, that is, learnt beliefs based on past experiences. If by your own admission you are simply no good at public speaking what you are in fact expressing is your sense of yourself.

Should you find yourself in a situation where you can't avoid speaking to an audience, say being asked to speak at a friend's wedding, you will probably endure sleepless nights in the lead-up to the big event, because of the emotions of anxiety you are feeling. You don't believe you can do this, or you believe that you will make a fool of yourself. Because your beliefs and sense of self don't support you in this situation, you will feel the stress and find it hard to take the necessary steps to prepare. These negative emotions will be paralysing. The chances are the speech won't go well or, even if it does, you will convince yourself that it was terrible and in the process reinforce the underlying limiting belief that you have of yourself.

Refer back to the MINDsense model. The results we produce in life, the outcomes we achieve, are always a direct reflection of what it is that we believe about ourselves and our life. This is the case because our beliefs determine what actions we take – our behaviour – and our actions determine what outcomes or results we achieve.

We will continue to explore these connections in more detail as we progress through the following chapters.

Newk's response

I wish Mike had been with me back in December 1963 when, as a 19-year-old, I played my first Davis Cup match for Australia. It was actually the Davis Cup final, one of the most important events in world tennis, and it was being played in Adelaide against our arch-rivals, the United States. Understanding Mike's MINDsense model at the time could have helped me change the outcome of the match!

Playing Davis Cup for your country is a totally different experience emotionally to playing for yourself, even a Wimbledon final. At Wimbledon, the umpire says 'Game Newcombe'; in Davis Cup they say 'Game Australia'. You are playing for your country, representing the nation and every citizen and tennis fan in it. You are continuing a wonderful proud tradition and all the efforts of those who have played before you.

The previous year I had been in the Davis Cup squad; however to have a chance of playing you need to be named in the 'team' of four players from which those who will take to the court to play are selected. When the final team was named, I was the surprise selection although not too many people – myself included – thought I would be chosen to play. In those days, the world's best singles players also played doubles, so they often played both the singles and doubles matches, which meant that often only two or three of the four team members were actually called upon to play.

The day before the matches, the two teams marched onto the court to conduct the draw. We lined up and faced the famous Davis Cup, which held the names of the players nominated by their captains to play. The players' names were drawn from the Cup and the pairings for the opening day's singles matches were announced. As a rookie and the youngest player by five years, I was sure I was not one of the names, especially as no one had said anything to me about playing. When my name was called out along with Roy Emerson to play singles for Australia on day one, you could have knocked me over with a feather!

Afterwards I asked captain Harry Hopman why he hadn't told me and he said, 'I just wanted to see the expression on your face.' Hop was known as a great tactician, but in my opinion he handled the situation badly.

The rest of that day before the first singles matches went by like a whirlwind and at no time did

Hop sit down with me to see how I was feeling or try to explain what I should expect emotion-wise the following day. That night it took me about two hours to go to sleep as I worried about all sorts of things, particularly being able to do justice representing my country.

I had to play Dennis Ralston in the opening match, a player I had beaten four weeks previously on the same court in the final of the South Australian Championships. This time in the Davis Cup final, though, it was different. There was much more at stake.

The first set was reasonably close, although I was very uptight, with Dennis winning 6–4. I got even tighter after that, losing the second set 6–1. My worst nightmare was being played out right in front of my eyes and in front of a huge crowd who had come to support me and the team. At the change of ends, Hop was appearing relaxed and confident but I knew inside he was having serious doubts about my ability to handle the extreme pressure of playing for my country.

Anger can be either a great friend or a destructive enemy and I used my anger at my predicament to kick-start my emotive and physical energy that day, winning the next two sets and taking the match into a fifth set. In a cliff-hanger, I lost the deciding set 7–5. I had given my opponent too much head start in that first nervous hour.

This was the biggest match of my career to date and I learnt some invaluable lessons. In fact, it started a practice for me of looking for lessons from my matches, a practice that stayed with me throughout my career and helped me to continue to develop and improve my performance. Never again did I give my opponent a huge head start due to my inability to control my emotions. I also learnt that day what a powerful ally positive anger can be. I witnessed the destructive power of the Negative Force and realised that I needed to recognise this enemy so that I would know when it was trying to enter my mind and body. This may sound a bit dramatic, but to defeat an enemy as powerful as the Negative Force you must really get to know and understand it.

I cannot emphasise enough how real this force is. No matter how knowledgeable and experienced you become, it can still overcome you unless you stay alert to the danger signs.

Some of the best advice I can give is that in the aftermath of a situation that did not come out well you should make an honest evaluation of where things started to go 'pear-shaped' for you and seek to understand why you started to think and act negatively. You will find that at a certain point you allowed the Negative Force to enter your body.

A prime example of this can be seen in major golf tournaments like the US Masters, where we have often actually witnessed young men leading the event slowly start to self-destruct simply because they failed to recognise, or didn't have the skills to recognise, that the Negative Force had made a successful attack on them. They were starting to choke!

As a consequence of the Davis Cup match, I began a habit of going through a dress rehearsal in my mind, usually about one hour before going onto court. I would picture my opponent and myself walking to the court, the umpire tossing a coin to see who served, the warm-up hit, followed by the start of play. In this way when I walked onto court I felt more comfortable with my surroundings and the people around me. I would also look into the stands and soak up the atmosphere and the emotions that were running there. After all, the fans are an integral part of the whole performance.

Mike talked about facing situations you have self-doubt about. A good dress rehearsal will certainly help to alleviate the doubt and improve your performance.

Mike's observations

How fascinating to hear from Newk about how he experienced his first real big-time match as a 19-year-old. Imagine yourself in his shoes for a moment and allow yourself to feel the emotions he would have felt as he walked onto centre court with so many people there hoping and praying for him to be successful. Feel the tension and the expectation. A couple of things stand out from Newk's response.

First was his ability to change his emotional state at the end of the second set. Down two sets to love, he was able to harness his 'positive anger' to kick-start a comeback.

What does he mean by 'positive anger'? This is not the anger we feel when we are in an argument with someone else, the anger that sees us fume inside with rage and burn energy. This is a different sort of anger, a reflective dissatisfaction with our situation that fuels an inner resolve to fire up and fix the situation, an emotional state that actually feeds us energy and helps us to lift our performance. When accompanied by reconnecting with your belief in yourself and your abilities and taking complete ownership of your predicament, this dissatisfaction creates breakthroughs. It is incredibly powerful if you can consciously create it!

Think back to your own experiences in life when you have found yourself completely dissatisfied with an area of your life and you have quietly resolved, with intensity, with a fire in your belly, to sort it out. That's what Newk is referring to here.

It is also critical to recognise that you have the power to change your emotional state from negative to positive at any time. Newk was able to force out the anxiety and nerves that were inhibiting his performance. To start with, he thought about his situation and rather than accept it he started going through his rehearsed and well-practised process of turning it around.

If we review this using the MINDsense model, we can see how his negative emotions affected his behaviour and impacted his ability to play his best tennis. The outcome, down two sets to love, was the result of this chain reaction.

In order to turn the situation around, he needed to change his emotional state from anxious to determined, focused, intense and hungry! To do this he needed to consciously reconnect with his inner belief about himself and reaffirm his sense of himself – to mentally connect with and reaffirm his ability to succeed. No sooner had he done this and his behaviour – how he played – improved and his best tennis emerged. He then gave himself the best chance to get the result he wanted.

Newk would probably have said to himself something like, 'This is ridiculous, I beat this guy here last month.' In the process of exploring this, he was able to re-engage his self-belief. The thought that would have emerged was probably as simple as 'I can beat him'. Having thought this and reconnected with his self-belief, he would have felt his emotions change. His resignation or despondency would have been replaced with determination and resilience. With this change in how he felt – his emotional state – would have come a change in behaviour. The increased focus and energy that positive emotions provide would have led to an improvement in his game that manifested itself on the scoreboard. This is the MINDsense model in action.

All too often I find the people I work with resigned to their situation. They accept their predicament and all that it will deliver, whether good or bad. Those who are able to continually develop and grow are those who are able to stop, organise their thoughts and challenge themselves to overcome their circumstances. The first response of the subconscious mind is one of acceptance, so we need to train ourselves to think differently and consciously challenge that first response.

Second, it is interesting to note the relationship that Newk has with the Negative Force, the force that has its roots in self-doubt and is expressed as anxiety or fear.

If we consider for a moment the origin of this force we will recognise that it can only be either external or internal. If it were to come from an external source it would need to be planted in us by that external source.

Of course that is not the case; the Negative Force comes from within us as we react to our situation, as we contemplate the circumstances we find ourselves in and allow ourselves to doubt ourselves. No one else can plant that doubt; it already exists within us.

This is not something we stop to think about; it is delivered by our subconscious mind as it explores our sense of ourselves relative to our circumstances. This unconscious sense of self is often described as our comfort zone. Whenever we head into uncharted territory – a place where our sense of self has not developed a frame of reference for us – we will often find ourselves feeling some amount of self-doubt and anxiety.

A maiden Davis Cup match in the final of this huge global sport is probably about as uncharted as you will find in world sport.

Newk treats the Negative Force as if it is an external threat. This is key in his ability to control and defeat it, because it means he is not fighting himself. It is almost as if he has tricked his mind. If he treated the force as coming from his own inner self, he would have to acknowledge his self-doubt and that he was part of the problem. This could lead to him questioning the strength of his inner self and potentially exacerbating any self-doubt.

I have seen many occasions where people start to question themselves as they experience self-doubt. 'Am I good enough? Am I capable of achieving this?' This questioning often leads to them believing less in themselves and the Negative Force prevails.

The way Newk deals with the Negative Force, it is not about him. By externalising it, he is able to strengthen his own sense of self as he steps up to take on this 'foreign invader'. He does not accept that the doubt is his; he acknowledges the Negative Force is the enemy and reaffirms his self-belief to push it away. Newk is going to beat it. His sense of self is strengthened as he takes it on.

Chapter 3

In the Beginning

Mike

One of the great joys in life is watching children at play in their first couple of years as they explore their world. They have a fascination with simple things like their hands and feet or sucking on some new object or gazing at some new image as they explore their world.

If you think about the world of a two-year-old, there are a number of wonderful factors at play.

First, they have no fear because they haven't learnt to fear. They have no inhibitions, nor do they give a toss about what others may think of them. They do not fear others' opinions. They have no limiting beliefs about themselves, nor a limiting sense of themselves. The world is just a great big, exciting opportunity waiting to be explored. We might call that state complete freedom.

This is how all of us arrive on the planet: pure, fearless, the perfect embodiment of a human being. The shame is that most of us only get to live in this blissful state for the first couple of years of our lives before it becomes 'polluted' by the experiences of our lives and how we deal with and react to them. In the process, these events and how we deal with them influence how we view ourselves and help to create the illusions of self that we become strongly attached to and associate with for the rest of our lives.

When two-year-olds look in the mirror, their view of themselves is simple and pure. There is nothing missing, nothing faulty, no imperfections. They don't look at themselves in judgement, or find fault with their appearance. They don't have an opinion on their height, the colour of their hair or their looks. Put quite simply, they just *are* and they don't see themselves as not enough or less than enough. Not ten feet tall and bulletproof, not perfect, they don't have all the answers; but they are enough, without question.

Now you are probably thinking that fear is useful as part of the response mechanism to threatening situations and that we need to have it in order to survive. You are right, of course; fear and adrenalin, fight or flight, are all useful physiological responses to our circumstances. However, how many times do you find your very survival threatened in a day, in a week, or in a year? Not to mention in a lifetime? Most of the things we are fearful of today are not in fact life-threatening at all. Public speaking, failure in business or what others may think of us are the things we commonly fear and not one of those will kill you. Imagine if you didn't fear them.

It does raise an interesting question, though. Why do we fear things that aren't actually life-threatening? If our life isn't threatened, what do we actually have to fear? What are we afraid of? Perhaps what your mind fears most is change and not being enough, whatever that is.

At some point in our infant lives, we are introduced by the actions of others to the concept of judgement and opinions. Up until that time, everything in our lives just *is*. We don't have an opinion on any aspects of life, they just are; not right or wrong, good or bad, beautiful or ugly, easy or hard, positive or negative. All are concepts involving judgement. Interesting, isn't it? Something that once 'just was', we now start to question. Is it good or not so good? Is it beautiful or ugly? Is it OK or is there something wrong with it? When once we were OK about the aspects of life, now we are not so sure. We become a little uncertain.

A two-year-old may look at their favourite doll and in their eyes and mind they will see this wonderful 'thing'. Perfect, desirable and without fault. It just *is*. And then they will hear someone express an opinion about the doll. An opinion that could be any one of the following: 'Such a shame it's old and falling apart', 'Look how cheap the eyes and hair is' and 'Gee, they could have made it better'. It's not long before the child also starts to question the doll and this once beautiful thing soon starts to lose its appeal. They become uncertain about the doll and what it 'should be'. They start to question whether the doll is enough.

At some point in our lives we will turn that questioning inwards. We start out in life not questioning whether or not we are enough because we just *are*, but as we grow up we experience judgement and the opinions of others and start to become uncertain about many aspects of life. As a child growing and learning, we take so much in and often we don't understand or know how to differentiate between the opinions and the advice that others offer. We find ourselves surrounded by a world of judgement; people's judgement of others, themselves and their environment.

The process of judgement is essentially the expression of an opinion about whether something or someone is what it should be, or whether it is good enough. As others in our lives express their opinions and judgement of everyday events we learn to question these aspects of life and become increasingly uncertain of how 'it is meant to be'. Their judgement may be of us or their opinion about us and we start to question whether we are what we should be or whether we are enough. Without understanding what is really going on we give too much notice to some opinions and become unsure of ourselves in the process.

As we go through childhood, we start to develop our sense of self and the events we experience in our early life have a big impact on how our perspective of ourselves develops. If we grow up in a world where people often judge us or express critical opinions of us or our actions, we may find ourselves believing that we aren't enough. If their judgement is about others, then we may compare ourselves to those being judged and find ourselves questioning ourselves against this 'benchmark'. We become unsure of ourselves and this lack of self-certainty translates to a lack of belief in ourselves. This resultant low self-belief leads to a lack of confidence and we approach life and our opportunities with uncertainty and hesitation. If we are surrounded by people who constantly encourage and praise our efforts and express their belief in us, who do not engage in constant judgement of the world around them, we will grow up not questioning or questioning less whether we are enough.

The impact of this process of questioning whether we are enough often stays with us for life. When you analyse what sits at the core of self-doubt, you will find that we are in fact doubting whether or not we are enough. When you analyse what sits at the core of our fear of failure, you will find the fear of what people think of us. Why would we concern ourselves so much with the opinions of others? It's because we use the opinions others have of us as a measure of whether or not we are enough.

What represents enough is different for each of us and it is generally based on one of two views: whether I am being who I think I am *supposed* to be or whether I am being who I *need* to be.

Who I am supposed to be is influenced by expectations. As I grew up in a very positive and supportive environment, the message I often heard was that I would be successful and significant. It is important to recognise that this was the message I heard, because it was not necessarily the intended message. I have since learnt never to assume that I know the intention of the person communicating the message.

I remember the annual Christmas lunch and the once-a-year get-together with relatives when an old aunt or uncle would express the view that no one needed to worry about Mike because he would always do well – well-intentioned and very supportive and encouraging expressions of encouragement that landed on a child like millstones. Why did I interpret the messages that way? Perhaps it was because my sense of myself and who I was supposed to be was developing and I didn't possess the skill or experience to be able to analyse the message.

As I look back now on my career, I find it both sad and amusing. There I was at 28, the CEO of one of Australia's premier sports, with my appointment heralded in the press as a watershed moment in the history of Australian golf, and yet I was still not enough. In fact if anything I was perhaps more fearful of failing and therefore not being enough – of not being who I was *supposed* to be, successful and significant. If I had not learnt the lessons I did in later life, I hate to think what I would be chasing now in an effort to prove my enough-ness. Prime Minister would probably not have been enough!

Some of us are driven by who we think we are supposed to be and others by who we think we need to be. Who I need to be is driven from a different perspective. Whilst who I am *supposed* to be is driven by expectation, who I *need* to be is driven by negative forces. It is the need to prove that the negative views and opinions others have of me are wrong and that I am in fact much better than that, and enough. Just watch me prove it! If we have grown up in an environment where we witnessed or experienced a lot of judgement, we are more likely to be less certain of ourselves and therefore have a greater need to 'prove ourselves'.

One is ultimately a need to prove that people were right and the other is the need to prove that people were wrong.

Over ten years of mentoring several thousand corporate executives from many of Australia's leading corporations, I have come to see that what sits at the core of their anxieties and fears, as it did for me, is the question of whether or not they are enough. Whenever people or circumstances appeared to me to threaten my being successful or significant, my stress or level of anxiety would spike dramatically.

In life I have found that there are three main areas

where people seek to prove their worth, their enough-ness. The first is through their achievements or results. If I achieve my monthly targets then surely I must be enough. If I am recognised for my achievements then surely that proves that I am enough. I have worked with many business people who are extremely focused and obsessed with getting great results at any cost and what has driven this has been their need to prove themselves. To prove to themselves and others that they are enough. Whilst this drive helps them to achieve, it is accompanied by the constant stress and anxiety associated with the contemplation of failing to achieve. They and others around them pay a high price for their drive to prove that they are enough.

Striving to prove that we are enough through the results we achieve is a never-ending game. We may work hard and with fierce determination to achieve a great result, but no sooner have we finished reflecting on our great achievement that we find ourselves having to do it all again. Next month's targets await us. There is no respite in this game.

The next way that many people attempt to prove that they are enough is through the opinions and approval of others. If others like me or approve of me in any way then I must be enough. The approval of others reinforces that my sense of myself is OK, it is enough. I see many people who are so caught up constantly seeking to please others so that they will be liked that they become prisoners to this never-ending pursuit. They worry about what people may think of the clothes that they wear or the way they do their hair. They are driven to always be doing things for others to the point that their own lives become a side show. If you seek to prove that you are enough through the approval of others you will always be chasing it. You may have that approval today but what about tomorrow? What will they think of me then?

The third way many people seek to validate that they are enough is through significance. The significance of their title at work or their position in the community. 'If I am significant I must be enough. If I am more senior than you then I must be more "enough" than you'. What generally transpires here is that maintaining the significance of the title takes priority over anything else. I must maintain my position at all costs. The 'overhead' associated with keeping up their position is usually accompanied by anxiety and stress as they constantly contemplate the 'impact' of losing their title, their significance.

People who seek to prove that they are enough through any or all of these three approaches – results, approval of others and significance – spend their whole lives pursuing enough without ever finding it. It's like looking for a great white shark in the forest. You'd be looking in the wrong place.

Rather than looking to prove we are enough through these pursuits we need to realise that we are already enough. We arrived on the planet the perfect embodiment of a human being without any doubt that we were enough. It was only through the experience of life that we came to see something different. It was only as others expressed opinions and judgement about aspects of our lives that we became uncertain of ourselves. Uncertain about whether we were enough. If you want to find it again so that you can find the peacefulness of life, look in the mirror. That's where it is. That's where it has always been.

There is a universal truth to this. We see it in every newborn baby. The state of purity, of unlimited potential. It never goes away; rather it just gets buried under uncertainty and doubt, under the opinions and judgements of others.

Consider it for a moment. If the notion of failure doesn't actually kill us, why do we have such a fear of it? Because it reconnects us with the question of whether or not we are whatever our measure of enough is.

To be able to tackle life and the opportunities it presents without reservation, it helps if you have certainty about who you are, don't fear failure and are not fearful of not being enough. Without the fear of failure, we are free to have a go and can express ourselves freely without inhibition. There are no opposing forces to our efforts and our energy and application can flow.

This must have been the world for Newk. From an early age he was free to have a go and not be held back by the fear of failure. He could take on board the lessons he was learning, the coaching he was being given, and continually improve his skills. Newk didn't need to prove to anyone that he was enough. He felt it and had no reason to question it. I am sure that the influence of his parents, particularly his mum, had a lot to do with this.

In all of the high achievers I have had the pleasure of working with over the years I have found at their core a simple trait that makes all the difference. I learnt to apply this to my own life and the change was profound. Put simply they are not uncertain about who they are. They have made choices about who they will be and are certain about themselves.

Newk's response

It's interesting to hear Mike talking about the fact that I see myself as being 'enough'. In general that is correct; however, as I took my journey through life, there were still plenty of lessons to be learnt.

I talked earlier about my first Davis Cup match and the emotions I went through. I lost both my singles during that match and in the days after I went through some strange emotions I had not previously experienced. Although I lost, I had fought very hard and had come close to winning each match. For some reason the public and media warmed to my efforts and took to me and I was treated like a hero. This was a little confusing to a 19-year-old.

Years later when I looked back on this time I realised that the following year had not been a particularly good one for me on the tennis circuit. My game advanced, but not nearly as much as I think it should have for all the work I put in. It's obvious to me now that while everyone was saying how great I was, and would be, my inner emotions were wondering if I was 'enough' and could live up to those expectations.

It would have been nice during that time to have someone talk to me about my emotions so I could tackle the problem head on. Obviously I eventually figured it out for myself, but there was definitely a nine-month period of doubt and uncertainty. I can't remember any defining moment when I decided simply to move on. I think it was more of a gradual awareness that I had to learn from the past and not dwell on it – to play in the present and plan for the future. Over that time I learnt to recognise that I was in fact enough and the results of my matches and the opinions of others had no bearing on that. I think in that place I was then free to play tennis without a lot of mental noise accompanying me for each match.

There is no doubt that the anxiety we feel about expectations we have of ourselves, or what we believe others may have of us, can hold us back from achieving our full potential.

I talk to kids a lot about this subject and it's fascinating to listen to their honesty once you get them going. I will get a 15-year-old up in front of 50 other kids and ask them to talk about a match they were playing where they held a big lead and finished up losing.

Let's say they led 6–2, 4–1 and then lost 6–4 and 6–2. So first I ask them how they were playing to get ahead and what was going through their mind. Then we pick it up at the 4–1 game and immediately you sense the room gets quieter and the 50 other kids are full of attention.

I ask, 'Did you change your positive and free-thinking ways to one of "Now that I have such a big lead, don't lose!"?' The answer is usually yes, so I explain that what has changed is that we now have a situation where they have started playing 'not to lose'. They are now playing negatively instead of positively. They are now playing with the fear of losing and this fear 'chokes' their performance.

I then ask if they started to think about explaining

the loss to coaches, parents and other people they were close to. We then get into a discussion of how the expectations of others can dramatically affect performance.

As we get into an in-depth discussion of emotions experienced as the match progressed, the other kids are hanging on every word, as this is not an adult telling them of a bad experience, but one of their own. We then talk about ways to recognise and acknowledge when the Negative Force is attempting to enter the mind and body, and some possible ways to drive it away.

The first and most important thing is to acknowledge to yourself that there is an impending problem that needs to be addressed, and quickly. Deep breathing followed by a large exhaling is one of the easiest ways to get the body to relax, and then follow this up by trying to smile. If you can't smile, it probably means you are too tense, so I suggest looking at someone and imagining they are an elephant or a rat, for example, and this should bring on at least a smile. The victim of your imagination will no doubt think you are a bit strange for smiling during a tense situation, but who cares? More than likely you will be in a more relaxed state and therefore able to perform at your maximum potential.

Mike's observations

As I read Newk's response, I couldn't help but think how useful the conversations he had with the kids would be for adults.

There are so many people trying to achieve their

goals and results at work who are hampered in their efforts by the fear that they carry with them. This could be fear of not making their targets, of not getting a favourable review from their manager, of not being liked by others, of failure. All are ultimately connected to the fear of not being enough.

How much better would we all perform if our minds were not occupied with this mental, negative noise? How much more appropriately would we behave and respond to our circumstances if the emotional state we felt was a mixture of confidence, determination, resilience, tenacity and purposefulness rather than fear and anxiety?

The pathway out of fear begins with consciousness. We need to stop and consciously think about our circumstances and plot a way forward. We need to reconnect with our inner strength. That strength has always been there since the day we were born, but has perhaps been hidden under the opinions and judgements of others.

We also need to look at our circumstances and consciously and honestly assess the seriousness of our situation. What is it that we fear and is it really worth that fear? Have you ever heard of anybody who died as a result of losing a tennis match, or whose very existence was threatened by not meeting their targets, or by the opinions of others?

Without fear, we are free to express ourselves more completely. Learn to lose it!

Chapter 4

Two Minds

Mike

One of the most important lessons I learnt in my own journey was triggered by a conversation with a Zen master and involved me contemplating my own unique existence and what it was that sat at the core of my very being. When I first explored this, I thought of my family and of the importance and need that we humans have for love as being the core of my existence, the very essence of my being. However, the present exercise requires exploring our world in isolation from others. What does my individual universe revolve around?

This is often a very difficult question for us to answer, because we are so closely connected to the answer that we are blinded by that closeness. To observe an object like a pen that may sit on your desk, you need to be separate from the pen. If you were the pen, without the ability to be separate you wouldn't be able to observe yourself. Similarly, we cannot observe ourselves unless we can stand aside from ourselves and from an external perspective look upon ourselves. If this is a difficult topic to understand, then stop reading and explore what we have talked about in your mind until clarity appears.

As human beings, we have the ability to separate from ourselves so that we can explore ourselves from an external perspective and sit in observation of ourselves. When you do this you realise that what sits at the core of our unique universe is our mind. In fact you can't even contemplate your very existence without your mind. Everything in your world, your perceptions, your experiences, your intuition and your movement originate from the mind.

We are so closely aligned with our mind as being who we are – this thinking, acting being – that we often have no separation from it. This thinking, acting human being is just who we are. This one mind and this one self are one and the same; but we need to delve deeper!

At various times in your life you may have had cause to stop and reflect on your thoughts. If you have ever been to a meditation class you have probably experienced the exercise of sitting quietly and observing the random thoughts as they flow in and out of your mind. In that moment you are observing your thoughts, you are in fact observing your mind.

The intriguing question for me when I first went through this exercise was, 'So, if I am observing my thoughts and my mind, what am I observing my mind with?' Think about it. As you quietly sit and observe your thoughts and your mind, what are you using to do this observation?

The answer is of course your mind. Your mind is observing your mind!

This introduces us to an interesting concept and the realisation that we in fact have two minds, or perhaps a split mind. In the exercise of observing our thoughts it is the conscious mind that is observing the subconscious mind.

The conscious mind is the real-time mind. It is the mind that we utilise in the present moment, the mind that we can control and direct as we engage it to work on what we are seeking at that moment. It is the mind that can explore opportunities and seek out new possibilities, the mind that in this exercise we instruct to observe the random thoughts of the subconscious mind.

The subconscious mind is the historical mind. It is the mind that is made up of the database of all our past experiences, the frame of reference we have developed based on our past life. It contains our historical sense of ourselves, our beliefs, our insecurities and our doubts, all of which were created as a consequence of these past experiences. Within this subconscious mind exists the perception that we have of who we are.

The subconscious mind operates without instruction. It is the mind that seemingly operates on its own, on autopilot. We do not consciously generate the thoughts of the subconscious mind, they appear as random thoughts that turn up uninvited, often, and seemingly with their own agenda.

It would seem that we have one mindspace but two minds that are competing for this 'processing power' or 'processing capacity'. Two minds are competing for the brainpower: the subconscious mind that is filling the mindspace with random thoughts and the conscious mind that we engage when we seek answers.

Occasionally we may express the view that we can't think straight. This would reflect the state we experience when the subconscious mind is generating a lot of random thoughts or 'noise' and there is little, if any, mindspace left for the conscious mind to engage. Sometimes we may express the view that we are of two minds about something. Perhaps in this moment the two minds have conflicting perspectives or thoughts about a matter.

As we observe our thoughts, we know that the conscious mind is observing the subconscious mind. Just as we discussed our ability to observe the pen, if we are able to observe the subconscious mind we know we must be able to separate ourselves from it to be able to observe it. We therefore know that with consciousness we are separate from our subconscious mind.

Now ask yourself, can you actually observe your conscious mind? Well, you can look back on what you have directed it to do but in the moment it is doing whatever you have asked it to do you are not able to observe it. It is operating in real time and we are only able to consciously process one thought at a time. You can't, therefore, generate and observe a thought at the same time.

To put this often seemingly complex topic into context, you will recognise that we see ourselves and our mind as being one and the same. Yet we are actually of two minds or a split mind and we don't differentiate between the two. We treat them as equals, yet one operates in real time, available to help us navigate the here and now, and the other throws up a random procession of thoughts, all of them generated in or connected to the past. Perhaps we need to be more discerning of which mind we listen to.

Put another way, we need to work out which one not to listen to. The conscious mind is concerned with this present moment and projecting us into the future, while the subconscious mind just wants to drag up the past.

The first step is to recognise the existence of two minds and through that to become more aware of our thoughts, their origins and their usefulness.

Newk's response

I learnt a lot about myself during my early years on the international circuit and many of the lessons I learnt occurred in the heat of battle on Centre Court, Wimbledon. It's under that intense electrifying pressure that one can easily lose focus as points, games, sets and matches slip away before you become aware.

In my fourth year, I lost to good friend Fred Stolle 7–5, 8–6, 6–4 after having set point in the first set, 4–1 in the second and 3–1 in the third. Suddenly I was sitting in front of my locker trying to remember what had happened and how I had lost those leads. Normally I would have vivid recall, as I had made a habit since 12 years of age of analysing my losses so I could try to plug the areas where my game was exposed, whether they were technical, mental or physical. In this case I couldn't bring focus to bear on how Fred overcame me, so I came to the conclusion that my mind had allowed itself to be caught up in the emotion and electricity of Centre Court.

From then on, I was constantly on alert should it start to happen again. Despite that I was caught off guard five years later in a quarter-final with Holland's Tom Okker, a player I had numerous close battles with. I led two sets to one and 5–0 serving in the fourth with new balls. At the change of ends, half the crowd left to get refreshments, as it was obvious the match would be over in a few more minutes.

I allowed my mind to leave with the crowd and within 12 minutes Tom had broken my serve three times, levelling the set at 5–5. People were starting to hurry back to their seats and the atmosphere was suddenly electric and alive with excitement.

The message to myself was quite clear: 'You can fret over what is going on, or you can play the next two games like your life depended on the outcome!' I decided to draw a line in the sand, put my head down, and won the next two games, but it took a supreme test of mind over circumstances to achieve. I quickly needed to engage my conscious mind to determine the course of action I would take.

I guess what I am saying here is not to be too hard on yourself if you make mistakes under pressure. Get conscious to your situation and turn the negative result into a positive one by learning your lesson and making sure it doesn't happen again. Had I not lost the Stolle match the way I did, I might not have had the strength and knowledge to hold off Okker's charge.

I lost to Laver in the final that year (1969) and won the following year in what was for me my favourite match. Before I get onto that, I want to talk about the year after (1971), when as defending champion I played American Stan Smith in the final.

My form was excellent and, after winning the first set 6–3, I was on top in the second but hadn't been able to break serve. At 4–4, while at the net I dived for a passing shot landing heavily on my solar plexus and stomach, knocking the wind out of me. Before long I had lost the second set, was down 4–2 in the third and feeling very tired. The temptation or subconscious response would have been to panic, but instead I engaged my conscious mind and tried to think logically about why I could possibly be tired when I knew I had done the training to play a four-hour singles followed by doubles and come up OK the next day.

I thought back over the match and realised that when I fell it had knocked the inner energy around inside my body and I had not spent time 're-energising' my body and mind. The instant and conscious decision was: 'I am going to lose this set, so don't worry about it and spend the next ten minutes deep breathing and re-charging the batteries. Stan will probably be very confident, so if I suddenly come back at the top of my game in the fourth set he will be taken by surprise.'

In the fourth set I led 5–4, 40–0 on serve and to that position I had not lost one point in my five service games. Stan won a couple of points from there but I served out the set and went on to win 6–4 in the fifth.

The critical stage of the match was the middle of the third set when I shut out everything and took a few minutes to figure out what had gone wrong and a plan to do something about it. I consciously thought about my circumstances and then thought about how I would respond. I didn't allow my subconscious mind to interfere.

The question I am often asked is whether there is one match in particular that I have fond memories of. As I achieved a lot more than I dreamed was possible, it's a tough question to answer, however the 1970 Wimbledon final with Ken Rosewall is the one that stands out for a number of reasons.

Playing Laver in the 1969 final, followed by Rosewall in 1970, was a great honour as I consider them to be in the top ten of all time. Back then, most people ranked them in the top four or five of all time.

Ken is nine years older than me and when I was a strapping 17-year-old he was kind enough to practise with me several times at Sydney's White City Club. Now here we were nine years later facing each other on the famous Wimbledon Centre Court. Up until 1968, tennis was divided into Amateurs and Professionals, with the latter being unable to compete on the international circuit, Grand Slams or Davis Cup. Ken lost Wimbledon finals in 1954 and 1956 and then turned professional in 1957, so he actually missed out on 11 years, or 44 Grand Slam events, and still managed to win eight of them.

I have always had an excellent rapport with the Wimbledon crowd, but I realised Ken would be the sentimental favourite, as I had been champion in 1967 but Ken was yet to wear the crown.

The first set went to Ken 7–5 and then I started to get on top, winning the next two 6–3, 6–2 and taking a 3–1 lead in the fourth. The crowd started to get involved as they cheered his winners and got excited about my errors. I allowed myself to get distracted by the change in 'atmosphere' and before I knew it Ken had won five games and the set 6–3.

Walking to the net for a change of ends, I was angry and frustrated with myself and the crowd. I had 60 seconds at the change to do something, so I said to myself: 'How badly do you want to win this?' The answer was in the positive! 'Well, if you really do want to win you need to go out on the court and put yourself into a zone. There will be a tennis ball, a tennis court, and someone up the other end. The crowd, umpire and everything else does not exist!'

I played like a man possessed in that fifth set, winning it 6–1. It seemed as if I knew where Ken's shots were going before he hit them and everything I attempted was successful.

When you win something that big, it takes a couple of days for the excitement to settle down before you have a chance to digest what it all means. Yes, I was proud of the win, but I was more proud of what I was able to accomplish during the 60 seconds when the Negative Force had occupied my body and mind. I had come a long way from the 19-year-old who lost the first two sets of his debut Davis Cup match due to fear and self-doubt about who he was and whether he would let down his country and teammates.

Mike's observations

These examples from Newk provide a wonderful insight to the power of consciousness and a positive and clear mind, which give us the ability to stop and think and then consciously develop a plan to help us to create the outcome we desire. It is a perfect example of consciousness used to overcome the circumstances and plot a path forward.

It would appear that Newk was not fearful of losing. While winning was clearly his desire, perhaps this was supported by the realisation that the match was not a matter of life and death. The outcome was not going to determine whether Newk was 'enough'. It was certainly not 'all or nothing'.

As we remove the fear associated with not achieving the result, we free ourselves up to be able to perform at our best. We are free to 'be' and this allows all the years of training and preparation to flow through uninhibited and for us to perform.

Of course the outcome of our endeavours, like a Wimbledon final, is not completely in our hands. We have an opponent or other external factors that influence our ability to get an outcome. In business it may be our competitors or other market conditions that we need to contemplate. In many cases, like the Wimbledon final, we may not have a lot of time to respond to our situation before the opportunity is gone and therefore the speed at which we can engage our conscious mind is critical to our ability to get the desired outcome.

Often in sport we see individuals or teams overcome by doubt and the fear of losing, so that they find themselves somewhat paralysed by the Negative Force, as Newk would call it. This creates so much mental noise that they seem unable to harness their conscious mind to navigate their way forward. They are overwhelmed and slowly sink under the weight of the situation. They choke!

I see the same happening in business on a regular basis. People become overcome by doubt and quickly lose belief in their own ability to succeed. Their subconscious mind fills the mindspace with noise and they lose access to clarity of mind. They can't engage the conscious mind to think their way to success. They don't recognise their competing minds and so do not understand what is taking place.

I see Newk's great strength being his ability to stop and think about his situation. He had trained his mind through years of practice to recognise the Negative Force and he understood what he needed to do to rectify the situation. He recognised the difference between his 'two minds' and was able to engage the conscious mind.

Chapter 5

The Role of the Subconscious Mind

Mike

As we consider the concept of dual minds or a split mind, it is interesting to explore the role that each plays in our lives and their various functions. What is their purpose? You will recognise that most people rarely stop to explore their thoughts. Most of us don't stop to think about the way we think. We let our minds run free and accept whatever thoughts come and go during the course of each day.

Perhaps we could learn a thing or two from the world of Formula One motor racing. Consider how they treat their high-performance vehicles. These highly tuned and very sophisticated machines could be compared to the human mind. In preparation for racing, many hours are spent on the test track. Each element of the car's performance is analysed and fine-tuned. Each element of its operation is scrutinised and opportunities for improvement are explored.

We may not want to take quite such a disciplined approach to our minds but what benefits could we enjoy if we were a little more curious and analytical, if we stopped occasionally to think about how we were thinking?

Have you ever stopped to consider the origin of your thoughts? Have you explored which of your two minds generates the most thoughts? Do you sometimes wonder why your mind seems so 'noisy'? What's going on in that mind of yours, where are these thoughts coming from, how many of your thoughts are actually productive?

As I encountered the world of people who are free to experience and explore life to its fullest, people who are constantly growing and expanding their horizons, challenging their comfort zone and living life to the max, l found that these are all questions that they *would* explore. On the other hand, those who are stuck in life, wondering why they can't get what they want from life, these are questions that they rarely seem to ask.

So let's examine these two minds that compete for our mindspace.

The conscious mind, our real-time mind, sits on the sidelines ready and willing to be called into action to contemplate whatever directions we give it. Ask a question of the mind and the conscious mind retrieves the answer or it logically connects different elements of knowledge we have acquired to determine an answer. If the conscious mind needs to go further and seek answers, it will guide us through that process until the answer is evident. Most importantly, the conscious mind does not obstruct us. The conscious mind does not appear to hinder us in our endeavours to expand our lives, or as we seek to grow by acting on new opportunities.

If we engage the conscious mind by stopping to think about something it will create the outcome that we seek. If we decide we would like a new car and create the conscious flow of thoughts that would lead us there then the car will become reality. The problem, though, is that the conscious stream of thoughts required is quickly interrupted by the subconscious mind with its own agenda. Without any conscious effort on your part, and seemingly out of thin air, thoughts flow through your mind: reasons why you can't have this new car or why it would be difficult to achieve.

The subconscious mind is the part of the mind that contains our past experiences and the various associations we have with those experiences. It is like the database of our lives. The different things you have come to believe about yourself and your life and the perspective you have of yourself are all tucked away in your subconscious mind.

Perhaps most importantly the subconscious mind often seems to hinder our growth. We find ourselves presented with opportunities and then battling thoughts that are either cautious, overly conservative, or simply negative about our prospects. These thoughts are not invited to the conversation; they turn up unannounced and we find ourselves listening to them or battling them.

We have targets to meet and outcomes to achieve and we find our thoughts consumed by doubt or apathy even when the reward for the achievement of our goals is significant. What if I don't succeed? What if I can't? We seem to get in our own way. We may be on the verge of victory, having performed our best, and then out of nowhere the thoughts of doubt appear and we find ourselves feeling anxious.

It would seem that most of the thoughts that wander around our mindspace are those generated by the subconscious mind. It randomly generates a lot of noise in our mindspace, little of it productive. As you go through each day, stop from time to time and ask yourself, 'Did I generate that thought or did it just randomly appear in my mindspace?' You may be surprised how many of your thoughts are random thoughts, products of the subconscious mind and its unexplored agenda.

Importantly, the subconscious mind takes up so much of our mindspace that it restricts the amount available to our conscious mind. At times like this, we struggle 'to think straight'.

To explore why the subconscious mind generates so much 'noise', we need to understand its function – why it exists in the first place and what its purpose or agenda is.

Those who have pursued the understanding of the subconscious mind from an academic perspective may feel inclined to dismiss my assessment as simplified or even naive. What I do know is that for ten years, as I have taught these concepts to others, not only have they been able to grasp the ideas but many have applied this understanding to their benefit. I was searching for simple and maybe I found what I was looking for.

Either way, if you consciously create a frame of reference for your mind, it will operate to that frame of reference. Why not then create a simple one?

The subconscious mind appears to operate with two objectives.

The first relates to perhaps the most important responsibility our mind has, management of our survival. Put simply, your subconscious mind is responsible for keeping you alive. It keeps you out of harm's way and warns you of impending danger. To do that, it seeks to keep us operating within the boundaries of what we know, of what is familiar to us. None of your actions to date have killed you, nor have any of your thoughts or responses to life's events. The chances are if you continue to act, think and respond to life the way you have so far in your life then nothing in the future will kill you either. The unknown represents uncertainty, a place of no guarantees – a scary place if you are seeking certainty. Have you ever wondered why humans resist change, the one constant in our lives? It's because it often represents uncertainty, a journey into unfamiliar territory.

Let's consider the following scenario. Imagine that you have been given a couple of toddlers to look after for the day, a couple of free-spirited 18-month-olds. Your primary task is to bring them back alive and well at the end of the day. We already know that at that age they have no fear, no limiting sense of themselves. Theirs is a world of great excitement and unlimited opportunity. Here is the challenge: the house you will be looking after them in has a five-lane freeway right outside the front gate, with trucks, cars, buses and potential danger written all over it.

Given these circumstances, with potential danger and harm all around you, what steps will you take to ensure the welfare of the children? To start with, you could lock the front gate, then the front door, in fact all the doors and the windows. If you were even more concerned, you might restrict them to one room in the centre of the house. By putting the house into 'lockdown', you would be creating an environment that is contained and predictable, an environment where you have certainty that everything is OK, that it is safe and no harm will come to the inhabitants.

This in essence is what our subconscious mind is doing to us every day. In order to manage our survival, our mind seeks certainty, familiarity and predictability. Look back through your life and you will see patterns in how you behave, patterns in how you think, patterns in how you respond to the events taking place in your life, and even patterns in the emotional states you experience. Patterns represent repetition, the same response in terms of how you think and act in the face of certain situations.

For instance, someone asks you to speak to a group of people and the emotional response is the same every time: perhaps anxiety, followed by thoughts of self-doubt. As you reflect on your responses to the events of your life, you will find a predictable pattern in terms of your thoughts, actions and emotions.

Your subconscious mind is happy when you are predictable because its ability to manage your survival in the face of life's challenges is made so much easier by this very predictability. Hence the term comfort zone – the zone of comfortable predictability, the zone of familiarity.

To maintain our predictability, our subconscious mind will take whatever self-definition our life experience creates for us and work to keep it in place. It will want us to stay true to the perception it has of who it is that we are. It will seek to maintain our comfort zone, our version of our beliefs and sense of self. I have conducted mentoring sessions with several thousand people over the past decade and I constantly hear them tell me who they are, both positive and negative:

'I'd love to play more golf but I am not a patient person.'

'I'd love to lose weight but I have no discipline.'

'That role would be perfect for me because I'm really good with people.'

'I don't care how tough the challenge because I'm tenacious and I'll get there.'

All of these are statements that reinforce the view that we have of ourselves. If you translate this back to the MINDsense model you start to see that the roadblock to us achieving what we desire in life has very little to do with external factors and so much to do with our subconscious mind and its view of ourselves.

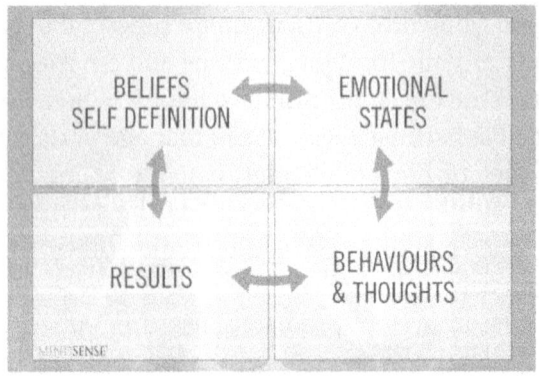

In order for us to be able to achieve new results in life, for us to be able to seize opportunities and create new outcomes for ourselves, we need to take the appropriate action that will generate or lead to the outcome. In order to take that action, though, we need to believe in the possibility of the outcome and we need to see ourselves (our self-definition) with the necessary attributes.

So here is the challenge. For so many people, their subconscious mind resists both the learning of new beliefs and any change to their sense of themselves. If either of those things changes, then our predictability is diminished. Hence we develop a perspective of ourselves in our childhood and our subconscious mind constantly reinforces that we are that person. Because we connect with only one mind, we accept it as real. We do not engage our conscious mind to challenge the subconscious thoughts.

Many of the statements people make about themselves, if not the vast majority, are not consciously created thoughts. They are the random thoughts of the subconscious mind that reinforce the perceptions we have of who we are.

Let's take the first example: 'I'd love to play more golf but I am not a patient person.' I asked the person who told me this if he had ever been patient in his life and he answered, 'Of course I have'. I also asked him how much conscious thought he gave to his first statement. Did he think about his patience before he made his comment? Interesting, isn't it? Without thought, he utters that he is not a patient person, yet when he stops to think about it he realises that statement is not true. It may be true that at times he had not demonstrated patience, but it is not universally true for his life.

At some subconscious level, his mind has become attached to the mental concept that he isn't a patient person. Perhaps it was a throwaway line from a parent when he was a toddler exploring a new game. The subconscious mind tucks this away in its database and then seeks to hold him true to this sense of self.

Now, in his adult life, he has the opportunity to play and enjoy the game of golf yet he seemingly can't get out of his own way to do so – not unless he thinks about it and uses his conscious mind to challenge the notions his subconscious mind has of him.

As the world around us goes through its never-ending and constant change, it is quite a challenge for most people to be able to change and grow with it. You would think the most advanced form of life on the planet would have learnt to deal with something as common as change and have evolved to deal with it better than we currently do.

I see this often in organisations which undertake a restructure or change of some sort. While some people embrace the change, most will struggle and in fact spend a considerable amount of time and energy opposing the change. Conversations with colleagues and in their own minds will be all about what is wrong with the proposed restructure, why it isn't necessary and the negative impact it will have on them. They seem to hold on grimly to the way it was and wish for it to remain so.

In effect, they are holding on to what it is that they believe about the situation and themselves. They are holding on to familiarity. At some point down the track, they will stop resisting and get on board with the change. However, they will have wasted weeks or months and now have even less time and therefore be under more pressure to get results on the board.

Others will simply choose to leave the organisation because 'it' is wrong and for many of these people this will become a career pattern.

We regularly hear terms like 'comfort zone' and how people would prefer to stay within that zone. We so often prefer to stay with the comfort of what we know and believe about ourselves and our world rather than explore new territories. Change takes us into new territory, but we have to let go first of where we are in life, of what we believe about who we are.

For some, letting go is almost impossible and they remain stuck, sometimes for life. They are stuck not being able to lose weight or quit smoking or change their approach or behaviour; because they can't become who they need to be to enable the change, they can't believe what they need to believe. They are stuck because their subconscious mind is running unchecked, constantly reinforcing who they are.

New outcomes or results require us to change, to let go of what we have come to think of ourselves as and to 'reinvent' ourselves. We have to learn to believe new things about ourselves, to consciously challenge the notions we have been accepting about who we are.

If we are forced to change by our environment, our resistance to change slows us down and creates internal friction that is a far from comfortable experience. Our results will probably suffer through this time when our energies are focused on resistance and not on moving forward. When change is being forced on us, we will at some point probably give up resisting and accept the change or the need to change. We learn to believe something new about our circumstances and ourselves and change becomes possible.

If you apply the MINDsense model to that process, you see the connection between results or outcomes and beliefs. The results that we are currently achieving in life, in fact the very way that we are experiencing life, is a direct reflection of what it is that we believe about ourselves and our circumstances. In order to get a new result, somewhere in life we need to learn to believe something new so that we can start to engage in different actions or behaviours.

A new behaviour is what is required to produce a new result. The definition of insanity is to do the same thing over and over again and expect a different result! In order to change our actions or behaviours, to start doing something new, we need to learn to believe something new about ourselves and our circumstances.

The problem seems to be that the subconscious mind invests a lot of time and energy defending what it is we have come to believe about ourselves and our world – defending our comfort zone – which is essentially what it is that we have come to believe about ourselves. Have you ever wondered why we do this, why we seem so intent on defending our beliefs, including our perceived limitations, rather than exploring new possibilities? We seem so focused on proving to ourselves and others that we are in fact who we think we are. We do this because this reinforces our predictability, one of the main functions of our subconscious mind as it seeks to keep us alive.

Our subconscious mind has also attached itself to some interesting concepts along the way that help it to resist change, concepts like our 'personality'. We accept our personality as the reason why we are who we are and also the reason why we can't change. Very convenient, isn't it, for the subconscious mind to have such an ally? Your personality is to such a large extent who you have come to see yourself as, and your subconscious mind has got you convinced this is fixed and unchangeable. Have you ever stopped to think about where this 'personality' of yours exists? Where in your physiology can it be found? The answer of course is in your mind. Your 'personality' is your subconsciously held view of your self. Your self-definition.

When I teach these concepts to business people, at all levels, the majority can grasp the simplicity of the model and understand the principles and the approach required. And then, with no conscious thought at all, they will say something like, 'It seems so simple, I bet it must be hard to do, though.' I say no conscious thought because they don't stop to think about what they are about to say, the words just come out, obviously delivered by the subconscious mind.

So why would the subconscious mind deliver such a thought? Quite simply, it's because if you believe it to be hard you are less likely to take on the task. If you don't take on the task, what happens? Absolutely nothing and you don't change. Advantage to the subconscious mind and its desire for consistent predictability.

I'll let Newk respond before we explore the other significant role of the subconscious mind.

Newk's response

In this chapter Mike has talked about growing up

and how the environment around you can influence how you think about yourself as you journey along your 'river of life'. Most of us have probably come to think that the safest course is always to stay on that big river for a nice safe journey. But safe often limits growth and opportunity and the true expression of our potential. What happens to almost everyone is that beautiful-looking tributaries offer themselves to us along the way. They tantalise with the offer of something extra, something special.

The key to remember is that it is in exploring these tributaries that we grow in life. In challenging ourselves to explore these new waters, we must step out of our comfort zone and in doing so we learn new things about ourselves and what may be possible for us. Ultimately we then move on from having a single main river to follow in life to having a complete river system. We will probably spend most time on our main river but with the freedom to explore further afield if we wish to.

Remember, if you do explore these tributaries, make sure you don't forget that the calm, peaceful waters of your big river will always be waiting for you; you just need to remember how to find your way back when you need to rest before taking on life's next challenge.

Earlier I talked a little about my early childhood and how I grew up in pretty nice and secure surroundings. Despite all that, I still had to develop my potential natural assets into real assets that would help me to achieve my life goals later on. I am talking here about what was going on in my mind and body on the emotional side, rather than physical things like hand–eye co-ordination, running, jumping, reflexes and so on.

I think I was born with what I call 'a fire in the belly', which can become one of your greatest assets when used in a positive way, and one of your greatest liabilities when it turns negative on you.

My mother was the one who recognised these traits and she spent a lot of time quietly working on my mental state when I threw a tantrum. This really helped me to understand the forces that were inter-reacting inside my mind and body. I guess Mike would say I was being shown how to develop my MINDsense.

There is no doubt in my mind that these early sessions with my mum played a decisive role in building a sense of self and inner strength and belief that would help me through some precarious moments during the rest of my life.

Wimbledon is the 'red carpet' event of world tennis. The English are not just good at holding such events, they are the best. Royal weddings, major sporting events, whatever it is and the bigger the better, they wrote the book on how to do it correctly for the rest of the world to follow.

My first trip there was when I had just turned 17 years old in 1961; I have only missed one year since and that was because of knee surgery. Before 1961, the tournament was not on TV in Australia and my knowledge was limited to newspaper articles and radio broadcasts. Nevertheless, listening on radio can really expand your imagination if the announcers are good at their job.

When I first walked into the grounds, it was exactly as I had pictured it in my mind. I was enraptured by the smell of history that emanated from the grounds, especially the Centre Court.

I noticed that above the entrance to Centre Court there were two lines from a poem: 'If you can meet with Triumph and Disaster, /And treat those two impostors just the same.' As I stood staring, I noticed to the left of me was the Honour Board of past Men's Champions and to the right the Women's Champions. At that time it went back over 70 years; today it is well over 100.

I was in awe but I wanted to know where the Triumph and Disaster poem came from, because it had immediately made so much sense to me that two competitors would walk under this archway and when they returned one would be rejoicing and the other trying to come to grips with a shattered dream.

I found out the lines were from Rudyard Kipling's poem 'If'. Here is the poem and I am putting it here because for me it embodies what Mike has been talking about in this chapter:

If you can keep your head when all about you
Are losing theirs and blaming it on you,
If you can trust yourself when all men doubt you,
But make allowance for their doubting too;
If you can wait and not be tired by waiting,
Or being lied about, don't deal in lies,
Or being hated, don't give way to hating,
And yet don't look too good, nor talk too wise:

If you can dream – and not make dreams your master;
If you can think – and not make thoughts your aim;

The Role of the Subconscious Mind

If you can meet with Triumph and Disaster
And treat those two impostors just the same;
If you can bear to hear the truth you've spoken
Twisted by knaves to make a trap for fools,
Or watch the things you gave your life to, broken,
And stoop and build 'em up with worn-out tools:

If you can make one heap of all your winnings
And risk it on one turn of pitch-and-toss,
And lose, and start again at your beginnings
And never breathe a word about your loss;
If you can force your heart and nerve and sinew
To serve your turn long after they are gone,
And so hold on when there is nothing in you
Except the Will which says to them: 'Hold on!'

If you can talk with crowds and keep your virtue,
Or walk with Kings – nor lose the common touch,
If neither foes nor loving friends can hurt you,
If all men count with you, but none too much;
If you can fill the unforgiving minute
With sixty seconds' worth of distance run,
Yours is the Earth and everything that's in it,
And – which is more – you'll be a Man, my son!

Did I learn anything from that first trip to Wimbledon? My first match was on Court 1, where I played the Swedish number one, Jan Lundquist, who was ranked about nine in the world. From a two-set deficit I won the next two sets before losing 6–4 in the fifth. In the doubles, Ken Fletcher and I got to the semifinals and in the quarters I had a real thrill playing on Centre Court for the first time with a five-set win over the number one British team. The atmosphere of a packed Centre Court was electrifying and I began a real love affair with the venue.

In my first Wimbledon, I had followed Kipling's advice and experienced Triumph and Disaster; it was to become my motto for the rest of my life. Over the ensuing years I have experienced every one of the situations in Kipling's poem and I can honestly say I believe I have been able to live up to each one. It didn't all happen at once, but as I have passed along the 'river of my life' I have learnt my lessons.

It was my seventh trip to Wimbledon before I experienced the ultimate triumph of winning the men's singles and entering the history books, although I had won the doubles twice before. Two years later, I lost in the final to Rod Laver – which was certainly no disaster given the greatness of Laver, but it was a really valuable learning experience.

As the champion, you hold up the trophy and parade around the court while 15,000 people cheer you, photographers can't get enough photos, and TV cameras follow your every move. As the loser, you sit in your chair observing everything that is happening and wondering what could have been. An old mentor of mine, Archie Punch, used to tell me: 'Winners are grinners, and losers can please themselves what they do because nobody really cares.'

After the Laver loss, I went on to win the singles the next two years but I never forgot the humility lesson of being the runner-up. Real contentment comes from learning to deal with the highs and lows, and realising that a spot between these two impostors is where you want to be.

'If you can talk with crowds and keep your virtue, /Or walk with Kings – nor lose the common touch'! An elite sportsman gets to meet many famous people and this in itself can be quite a 'heady' experience. One can start to forget the more important things in life, like real friends and family.

George Bush Snr has been a good friend for many years and I thought it was pretty neat when Angie and I spent Labor Day holidays at their Kennebunkport holiday house when he was Director of the CIA in the mid-1970s. We also attended his Presidential inauguration in 1989.

I have always been wary of this situation and fortunately my wife shared the same values. My friends of today are the ones I have had for 20, 30, 40 and 50 years. Of course, I have friendships with famous people in the movie business or politicians, but I have never gone out of my way to nurture these friendships.

I love all of Kipling's poem and one of my favourite parts talks about forcing your body to go beyond what you thought you were capable of. See if you can pick the four lines I will be referring to in a coming chapter to help explore where I had an experience in a Grand Slam final that took my body where it had never been before.

Mike's observations

At different stages of life, people will appear who are capable of teaching us. Sometimes it is in childhood, sometimes as teenagers and even as adults. Perhaps it is not the appearance of the teacher that matters, though. In the Zen world there is a wonderful old saying for this: When the student is willing, the teacher will appear.

I was reminded by my Zen master, Roshi Kitabu Turner, that in life there are teachers everywhere; the challenge it would seem is whether or not the student is willing.

At a young age Newk had his mother, as most of us do, as his teacher. Her wisdom did not fall on deaf ears, though. The strength of their bond, of their connection, ensured that he wanted to listen and learn. Later in life Newk had other teachers, people like his mentor Archie Punch, to guide him.

There is a great lesson in this for each of us and it is the preparedness to listen and to be taught. Many people I work with are too busy parading as know-it-alls trying to convince everyone that they are complete, that they are enough. What more is there to learn if you already know it all? There is certainly no room for a teacher, nor any willingness to embrace one. We need to recognise the importance of humility or vulnerability as a facilitator of growth.

Newk's approach to learning and growing highlights a trait I have found in every *content* high achiever I have met, and I emphasise the word content because I have met many high achievers who are far from content. It is the trait of humility. There is the recognition that we don't have all the answers ourselves and that there are others who are there to help us on our way. There is an openness to exploring new ideas, the curiosity to seek the advice of others.

Newk's mother would have been no help without his preparedness to explore and learn. Those wise and talented people he befriended on his journey would have been of wasted value without Newk's humility that allowed his inquisitive mind to find new and improved ways to approach life.

Some of the lessons Newk learnt from his mother probably came from such conversations as those lasting ten minutes in the car on the way home from a local junior tournament. Nonetheless, they were lessons that would prepare him for triumph on Wimbledon Centre Court. Imagine if he had ignored her words!

Because of Newk's humility and consequent ability to keep learning, he was able to continually learn to believe new things about himself. Over time his sense of self would also have strengthened. Each time he learnt something new about himself, his game or his approach and then applied that learning, he would have grown. Each year on the tennis circuit he would have grown in belief and ability until that wonderful day when he claimed the first of his Grand Slam singles titles. His career became one of continual improvement and growth that culminated in the world number one ranking.

To continue to challenge what you believe about yourself and your potential is not an easy process. Each time you do it, you are stepping out of your comfort zone, so by definition it is an uncertain time. Along with humility, it requires courage, but then that's who Newk sees himself as.

At the core of Newk's approach was a high level of consciousness. He refers often to how he stopped and thought about things that were happening in his world. His conscious mind analysed his triumphs and his 'disasters' and sought to find the lessons.

The subconscious mind seeks to reinforce the sense of self that we have developed to maintain our predictability. Operating within this sense of self is familiar territory. This is true whether your underlying sense of self is strong or weak. If that sense is that you aren't capable or enough, you will find proof that you can't deal with life's challenges without a struggle. If your sense of yourself is strong, you will probably do what Newk did, seek to explore your thoughts and grow, because that's just who you are!

Chapter 6

Subconscious Self-Validation

Mike

In Chapter 3 we explored the development of our sense of ourselves through our childhood, including the impact of our insecurities and doubts and particularly the notion of how that leads to us being uncertain of whether or not we are enough. If you observe a young child, though, you will notice that they don't question whether they are enough. They don't stand in front of a mirror and find fault with their height or weight or hair colour. The uncertainty that we are enough is something that we are introduced to at a young age as we learn from those around us the concept of judgement or the expression of an opinion.

Up until a certain age, everything in life just *is*. We then encounter the judgement and opinions of others early in life and from that we start to question whether things are good or bad, easy or hard, enough or not enough, and we are often not sure of the answer. Sometimes we would have found ourselves as the focus of others' judgements and opinions and soon we start to reflect inwardly and question, for the first time, whether we are enough. We become uncertain of ourselves. We see other people observing things or people in life that up until that time we saw as 'just being' and through their opinions or judgement questioning whether they are good enough or what they are supposed to be. We start to do the same thing, including questioning ourselves and becoming unsure about whether we are enough.

Consider what it feels like each time we find ourselves doubting whether we are enough or whether we are who we are supposed to be or need to be; when we are unsure of ourselves or questioning our own capabilities or contemplating our own perceived inadequacies; if we are unsure whether people like us or not; if we wonder whether we can live up to the perceived expectations of ourselves or others, or we fear being a disappointment. Uncertainty about ourselves and who we are is, for some, a lifetime curse – it doesn't feel good to be uncertain.

All human beings strive to see themselves as enough, to feel a sense of belonging, to feel worthy and valued, to be accepted by the community. At the very core of our being is a need for acceptance and connection, the need to be enough. With that, we feel good about ourselves, in a state of emotional wellbeing. A level of harmony exists.

On the other hand, our uncertainty about ourselves and the contemplation of our limitations and weaknesses, or the pressure to live up to expectations of what enough means to us, has just the opposite effect. It often leaves us feeling devalued and disconnected. We hardly feel good about ourselves when we feel this uncertainty and contemplate these perceived weaknesses. There are areas of disappointment in ourselves or our lives, the disappointment that we are not as 'enough' as others. We have feelings of doubt when we think about what we should be able to do or want to do or are expected to do.

Most, if not all, of this is happening at a subconscious level. These are not thoughts we are generating consciously; they are thoughts that seem to just turn up. And sometimes they seem to generate a lot of mental noise. Usually these thoughts are also accompanied by a change in emotional state. Have you ever wondered why you suddenly feel anxious, angry, or stressed? Have you wondered what caused how you feel to suddenly change?

If you were to explore this using the MINDsense model as a reference, at the core you will find that these emotional changes occur when your sense of yourself is being challenged by your circumstances or environment; perhaps your perceived inadequacies and self-doubts have been awakened. Your core being is now being challenged. Your beliefs and self-definition are under threat. Whether you are enough is being questioned or challenged.

Contemplate your monthly sales target and consider not achieving it. Think about having to speak at a business meeting with senior executives. Worry about the putt on the 18th green to win the side bet or whether you will make it on time to pick the kids up from school.

Why do any of these things often seem to bring negative emotions, particularly worry or anxiety, into play? It's because they bring doubt about whether we are enough. They connect us with the feelings of uncertainty and hurt we experienced when people doubted us or questioned whether we were good enough or capable, when our efforts or outcomes were being judged by others. When our sense of self is challenged, we will find ourselves feeling anxious.

Contemplation of not being enough brings with it pain. In other words, our ability to be enough is being challenged. For some people with little belief in themselves, life is experienced in a constant state of anxiety as they and others constantly remind them that they are not enough.

When this happens, we don't feel good about ourselves. We are in essence questioning our self-worth and the anxiety we feel can be debilitating. At this point the subconscious mind steps in to fulfil its second major function, to help us to feel good about ourselves and to restore the emotional balance. This process is going on literally hundreds of times every day as the circumstances we find ourselves in or think about and our self-definition interact.

The most common way for our subconscious mind to restore the balance, to help us to feel good about ourselves, is through affirmation and being right. It is the perfect expression of self-worth. Any time that I am right, I am OK. I am affirmed and I am enough. I am restoring the balance and my sense of self. I am worthy.

Contemplate for a moment how it feels when you are right about something.

The opinions that I express about everything and anything are part of this process. An opinion is something that I am being right about, whatever that opinion is. Whether the opinion is a positive one or a negative one, it is something that I am being right about. Many of the opinions we express don't lead to anything in particular, they are simply a verbal expression that comes and goes without any impact on anything:

'Could you believe the outfit Mary wore last night?'

'That pothole in the road should have been fixed by now.'

These opinions on their own will rarely alter anything (the outfit Mary wore is now history, the pothole remains in the road), but through the process of expressing these opinions we subconsciously reinforce our sense of self through being right!

If you explore your own thoughts and responses to daily life you will realise that your opinions on their own are innocuous, impacting neither positively nor negatively. There are some however which serve only to trap us. These are the opinions we express to ourselves about ourselves – the constant reinforcement that this is who I am which ensures we remain the same predictable person.

The subconscious mind will look for anything to be right about. It isn't choosy. Even being right about what I can't do will suffice, as will being right about who it is that I think I am. This is what I call the mind trap.

The opinions and judgements that we express are rarely consciously created. When was the last time you consciously thought to yourself, 'Gee, I haven't expressed an opinion on anything for a while, it must be time for me to find something to have an opinion about'? We rarely do. Opinions, and for that matter judgements that we make, are mostly thoughts delivered from the subconscious mind. They are thoughts that we are right about and that momentarily reconnects us with being enough.

In my work, I have found that people who are

the least certain that they are enough, those with the strongest need to prove they are enough in the face of their self-doubts and insecurities, will be those who are the most opinionated and judgemental in life. And none of it is conscious. It is the subconscious need to restore the feel-good balance that comes with being enough. However, it creates a lot of noise and not necessarily any worthwhile outcomes.

Why are they often the least certain that they are enough? Often it's because they have grown up in a world of opinions and judgement where enough is questioned and so they have become uncertain about whether they are enough. It may be that, because of expectations, they have come to think that to be enough they are supposed to be significant and successful.

This is a process that we human beings seem to have perfected. Have you ever witnessed any other form of life engage in the process of judgement? Have you seen a dog judge any aspect of life? Of course not. Like the toddler, for them life 'just is'. They don't sit there and judge what you are wearing out on a Saturday night. The process of judgement is something that would appear to be unique to us humans and it rarely serves us well.

Through this process of judgement we start to develop a sense of how we fit into that world. Are we good-looking? Are we intelligent and capable? Of course others will express their judgement and opinions of us in each of these areas and our sense of self starts to take shape, along with our insecurities and questions and doubts about whether we are enough.

If on balance we have more positives than negatives in our sense of self, we will generally feel capable and have sufficient belief in ourselves to be able to have a go in life. If the balance favours the negative, we are more likely to be reluctant to challenge ourselves, preferring the backseat in life and wishing we were more capable. We are of course already capable enough; we've just come to believe something else!

Consider the person who has low self-esteem. Expressed another way, they don't have a great deal of belief in themselves. In their opinion, theirs is a world full of things they can't do, or one where crappy things happen all the time, or where they are not good enough to deserve good things. How do they get to feel good about themselves when they exist in this state? Quite simply, they develop opinions and stories to justify why they can't achieve the things they want. They develop stories that explain why their world is as it is. In every story they create, they get to be right and in that moment of justification they get to feel good about themselves. They are momentarily enough.

The problem is that the crappy situation remains. They connect with one mind and do not realise that their subconscious mind has created the trap and is maintaining it. They haven't learnt to engage their conscious mind to escape the trap. They don't recognise that their subconscious mind is caught up in constantly being right about what's wrong with their life and constantly being right about who it is that they have come to think of themselves as.

As we develop our beliefs and our sense of self, our subconscious mind looks for evidence to support those beliefs and it casts a net in search of this evidence to maintain our predictability. If we go looking for something, the chances are we will find it and our subconscious mind is continually looking for evidence to support our beliefs, evidence which it always seems to find.

This process makes change very difficult, because change or growth requires new beliefs or a different sense of self and our subconscious mind seems more intent on proving and locking in the existing beliefs, being right about what is and who we are.

Consider someone who is significantly overweight. After several attempts at losing weight without success, they start to believe that they can't lose weight and that being overweight is just the way it is for them. Then the brain starts looking for evidence to support their belief that they 'can't' and in the process it maintains their predictability.

Listen to the reasons they will give you on why they can't lose weight: It's genetic; I haven't got any willpower; I'm depressed and I can't stop; I've tried everything and nothing works; I've got a sweet tooth; diets don't work for me.

If this is a conversation that often takes place in your mind, your subconscious mind has probably already started defending. The voice in your head is telling you without any prompting, 'What would he know? He doesn't understand.'

Just consider this: what's the voice in your head, your subconscious mind, doing? It's locking you into your current limiting beliefs and sense of self and as a result it is locking out for you the possibility of finding a way to achieve your desired outcome – to lose weight. It's investing more in the story about why you can't rather than how you can! This is your subconscious mind at work being right about who you think you are! An affirmation that feels good but also traps you.

These reasons seem perfectly valid but all just support the beliefs about why you are overweight. The more evidence you find for why you can't, the further away you move from being able to achieve your desired outcome. The reality is you can't achieve the result you want because you don't have beliefs that support this desired result. Your beliefs support the opposite and your subconscious mind keeps affirming these beliefs.

It would seem that the trade-off is between getting what we want, losing weight, or being right about why we can't. The subconscious mind opts for the latter because with that it also gets to fulfil the first function of maintaining our predictability.

Consider the loop that many get trapped in. As a consequence of our life experiences we all have uncertainty and self-doubts of some kind or other. Other people in our lives have doubted us and put us down in our childhood and others may have questioned our ability and raised uncertainty for us about whether we are enough. Over time, we may also have come to question ourselves and become uncertain about whether we are enough.

Because of our doubts and uncertainties, some challenges or opportunities in life appear beyond us and we may find ourselves feeling quite anxious as we contemplate them. In these moments of uncertainty, we don't feel good. The subconscious mind steps in with its two desires – the first to help us feel good about ourselves and the second to maintain our predictability. It achieves both simultaneously by developing a story about why we can't achieve the desired result or why it will be difficult, a story where it gets to be right because it confirms with certainty who we are. And when we are right it feels good because it momentarily confirms that we are enough while simultaneously locking in our sense of self and maintaining our ongoing predictability.

The more attached we are to a belief or to our self-doubts, the more we accept the thoughts of the subconscious mind, the more evidence seems to appear to support that self-view and the more the subconscious mind selectively uses that evidence to support and confirm our sense of self. The more the subconscious mind invests in creating and protecting our story, the more we lock out listening to alternative viewpoints. The subconscious mind focuses more on finding and letting in supporting data and in being right and it locks out other options. In this space, we lock out the possibility of finding a new way; there is no chance of a new possibility. It's very 'closed-minded' and limiting, but very predictable.

All of this self-validation takes place subconsciously. We don't consciously create these thoughts. The noise associated with these self-validating thoughts seems to overpower the mindspace and our effectiveness diminishes. There is less room for the conscious mind and too much 'automatic noise' going on for us to think straight and we quickly become overpowered by the subconscious mind and get stuck.

This is because we have lost our connection with being enough, the enough that we arrived into life with that was lost under the weight of others' opinions and judgements. Those opinions and judgements were expressed by others in their own subconscious search for validation, from their own subconscious need to reconnect with their enoughness. The problem is that we allowed their opinion to become true.

The unfortunate aspect of the human condition is that we pass this mind-sickness down from one generation to the next. Some don't succumb to it, though, and they are able to express themselves with more freedom in life, play a bigger game and achieve all that they wish.

Newk's response

In my experience of professional sport, the people who make it to the top are usually pretty sure of themselves, but that doesn't mean it's been an easy road. Along the journey to the mountaintop many tough questions are asked and not always answered in the correct way.

Roger Federer is one of the greatest players ever to grace the courts, but it took him four years of Grand Slam events before he found the necessary ingredients inside himself to win one. Until that time he was this multi-talented player of real genius who could put it together over one-week tournaments but didn't have the belief and mental stamina to last the two weeks and seven matches of Grand Slam tennis.

Two months before Wimbledon in 2003, he lost a match in Hamburg because he got angry and frustrated with himself. He made a decision to stop doing this to himself, won Wimbledon and the rest is history.

I guess Mike would say he was validating the negative aspects of himself as he judged and was critical of his own performance that day. His anger and frustration was Roger judging himself and expressing that his play wasn't good enough. Ultimately though he needed to understand who he was and then decide who he wanted to be.

Grand Slam tennis is real pressure and so is Davis Cup. In a way it is more pressure than playing for yourself, because you are representing your country, teammates, family and yourself. Under this sort of pressure even those with the strongest self-belief can begin to doubt.

In Davis Cup the team captain is allowed to sit on the court and advise the player at the change of ends after every two games. This can be a good or bad situation depending on the trust and relationship between player and captain.

From 1994 to 2000, Tony Roche and I were coach/captain of the Australian Davis Cup team. Tony and I had travelled the world together as teenagers, played Davis Cup and won for Australia, won 12 Grand Slam doubles titles, were rated as one of the best doubles pairs of all time, still lived close to one another and, best of all, our wives were very good friends. In our seven years of running the team, we started off with a group of young men who didn't really think they could win a Grand Slam or become the best team in the world.

We told them their bar was way too low, that ours was much higher; the journey would be tough but if they wanted to come along for the ride we would help show them the way to the mountaintop. There were heartbreaking losses and some satisfying wins along the way and after five years we became the best team in the world.

It was the despairing losses we had along the journey that actually made us such a strength. After each one, we would say to the team, 'We have been knocked down to our knees. This is a test of your character; when you stand up make sure you are standing taller than when you were knocked down. Tony and I are used to being winners and if you choose to stand taller we will be with you every inch of the way!'

To win the Davis Cup you have to be victorious in four matches over the year. In our sixth year we won four matches on four different continents (Africa, North America, Australia, Europe), on four different surfaces, and due to injuries never had the same team twice.

Along the way, we refused to accept that we were anything other than capable of being the best, that our stumbles were simply opportunities to learn from and grow. Together we validated ourselves around our strengths to such an extent that we could not be stopped. Here are three stories that happened along that journey that will show you how under extreme pressure, with a little help and a push in the right direction, the mind can be altered to turn a totally negative situation into a positive one:

1. In 1996 we were playing Japan in Osaka at a beautiful new outdoor stadium seating 6,000 people. The opening match was a young Japanese guy who hit

two-handed on each side and was ranked 253 in the world. Playing for Australia was Todd Woodbridge, one of the world's great doubles players. Todd had only been chosen to play singles the year before, losing both his matches in a heartbreaking loss to Hungary in Budapest. Todd was the better player by a long shot but the losses against Hungary were playing heavily on his mind.

He led 5–3 in the first set before losing it 7–6, promptly lost the second set 6–3 and pretty soon was down a service break in the third set at 2–1. As the players started to change ends, I pondered what I could possibly say to Todd that would help him rediscover who he really was so he could win the match. Towards the end of the second set at the change of ends he had looked at me as he tried to drink a glass of water and said, 'Look at my hand shaking; I'm falling apart!'

He slumped down in the chair and put a towel over his head. I could almost hear him thinking, 'I've let down my country, family, friends and myself; I'm a failure, I'll never play Davis Cup again.'

It occurred to me that the big picture of winning the match had become too much for Todd to digest and he needed to start focusing on a much smaller goal. My challenge was to work out how to get the message across, given that I only had 60 seconds during that change of ends.

I needed eye contact so I said: 'Todd, I need you to look at me.' He removed the towel and I am sure he was thinking I was going to give him the big speech about what he needed to do.

Instead I said: 'Do you realise what has happened

here? Two hours ago when you walked onto this court you knew, your opponent knew, your teammates and his knew, the 6,000 people here and those watching on TV knew, that there was no way he could win this match. Now we sit here two hours later and all those people know there is no way *you* can win this match.'

Todd looked at me like I was a bit crazy but I could see he was wondering where I was going with this.

'So don't you see how the situation has reversed? You no longer have to win, everyone now expects him to win, so all the pressure is now on his shoulders, not on yours, and I promise you this, Todd, if you just break his serve once he will be destroyed.'

Recognition of these facts dawned on Todd; I could see it in his eyes and the way he got up from his chair walking tall onto the court with a real purpose in the walk. The big picture which had been playing havoc with his mind had disappeared. He now had one small goal to achieve, to break serve once.

He started playing like Todd Woodbridge, broke serve at 5–3 and won the remaining three sets 7–5, 6–2, 6–2.

The lesson here was to not let the big picture consume you, to not get ahead of yourself, to stay in the present and take one focused and conscious step at a time. I needed Todd to stop beating himself up with self-criticism of his performance, to stop being right that he was a failure. Then I needed him to focus on something else that would actually contribute to getting the outcome that he wanted – breaking his opponent's serve.

2. Pat Rafter came onto the world tennis stage in 1993

as a 19-year-old with great athletic ability. By year's end he had climbed to 20 in the world and huge expectations were put on his shoulders by the Australian media and public, hungry for a new champion.

Things went okay during 1994 but 1995 began a slide so that by January 1997 his ranking sat at 63 in the world. At the Australian Open he lost in the first round to Albert Costa and voiced the opinion to Tony and myself when he came off court that he no longer believed he could match it with the world's top 20. We believed Pat's ability to be a top player was there, he simply no longer believed it himself, or in my mind he had lost what I call his 'warrior mentality', that ability to let his great natural instincts take over and not over-think the situation.

Two weeks after the Open, we played France at Sydney's White City Stadium and we chose Pat to play. He was scheduled first up against Cedric Pioline, ranked nine in the world and the hero of France when they won the Davis Cup the year before in 1996.

After losing the first set 6–3, Pat quickly went ahead 5–1 in the second set. Then something changed and he started to doubt himself, lost serve twice, and after leading 4–1 in the tiebreak lost it. He headed to the chair very despondent, slumped into it and said, 'Newk, I'm sorry, that's the biggest choke I have ever seen.'

Up until this stage I wasn't really sure what I would say. I felt a bit lost for words. Then out of nowhere I suddenly lost it and started telling Pat in a very loud voice, 'You don't have time to feel sorry for yourself, because we've got another three hours to spend out here and at the end of that three hours we will have buried Pioline so far under this court they will never find him. To do this, we are now going to begin a war of attrition and to win this war you are going to have to dig deep down inside your belly to rediscover the ball of fire that's buried there!'

The umpire called time and I followed him onto the court yelling about the war of attrition and the terrible things we were going to do to Pioline. I should add that I was also using some pretty bad language, as I figured I needed to shock Pat and bring the situation down to a real gutter fight.

He started to play like Pat Rafter and at 2–3 had a service game that went for 11 deuces while he saved seven break points. When he won the game, he pumped his fists in the air, I was out of my chair pumping back at him and I knew then by the look in his eyes that he was going to win. He had found that 'ball of fire' down in his belly, rediscovered his warrior mentality, and had drawn a line in the sand that said I'm not going back.

He won that match 6–4 in the fifth set. Eight months later he won the US Open and he was firmly implanted in the world's top ten.

Based on Mike's last chapter, I guess you could say Pat had been searching for two years to work out who he was, something he had lost due to the expectations of outside forces and perhaps engaging in negative self-validation. Doubt was creeping in and he was probably spending too much time questioning his ability and in the process validating to himself that he wasn't good enough.

In the end, the answer lay deep inside himself and he proved to be man enough to dig that out under extreme pressure. He stopped being right that he wasn't good enough and started to believe in himself again. In the process he probably developed a much stronger view of himself. He reconnected with strength.

3. Lleyton Hewitt at 15 had been invited into the team in 1997 as a hitting partner and had witnessed first-hand Rafter's fightback over Pioline. Two and a half years later in July 1999 he played alongside Pat to defeat the United States in Boston. He was on his way! In December of that year he was the spearhead of our team as we defeated France in Nice to become the world champion nation.

Twelve months later we were in the final once again, this time meeting Spain in Barcelona. It's tough playing overseas in Davis Cup with extremely paro-chial crowds and the Spanish crowds were among the most vocal. You get the feeling you are in a bull ring and you are the bull.

Four months prior to this match Lleyton had deve-loped some breathing problems which had hampered his ability to do the usual amount of training. He was scheduled to play the opening match against Al-bert Costa, a fiery competitor who played every point as if his life depended on it. As Lleyton played the same way, this promised to be an epic encounter with no prisoners taken. We had 1,000 supporters there but we knew they would be howled down by 13,000 Spaniards baying for blood.

Shortly before we went onto the court I said to Lleyton: 'You know this is going to be a very physical encounter and because you haven't been able to do the normal amount of training you could start to feel really tired around the two-hour mark. As soon as you start to feel your body going, you have to let me know and I can help you find a way to recover quickly.'

About two and a quarter hours into the match, with every point becoming a battle and the score at one set all and 3–2 to Costa, the players changed ends. Lleyton slumped into his chair, I handed him a glass of water and his hand was shaking so badly the water was spilling over the side. He looked at me and said, 'I'm buggered', which was true as his whole body was shaking.

Now was time to see how strong the trust was between us. I said, 'Sit back in your chair, try to relax your body and take a deep breath.' Remember we only had 60 seconds on the changeover. 'Your body is full of negative energy and we need to get rid of it. Take a very deep breath, close your eyes and as you breathe out imagine you are blowing all that negative rubbish out of your body, up above you is the clearest blue sky you have ever seen and you are now inhaling that clear air into your body which is full of powerful positive energy.' This was all a supreme test of imagination for Lleyton, as it was wintertime and we were indoors!

We had time to repeat this three times before having to return to the battle. I followed Lleyton out to the court and above the screaming partisan crowd kept telling him he was now the strongest bastard that ever lived and could run forever.

Lleyton lost that set, but we repeated the breathing routine every change of ends until, at the end of four and a half hours, he served for the match at 5–4 in the fifth set. The drama was not over as he promptly fell behind 0–40 on serve, only to win the next five points and the match. It was one of the most heroic performances ever by an Aussie in Davis Cup play.

What I had done was show Lleyton a way out of the dilemma he found himself in, and in doing so he discovered that his body was capable of doing amazing things if he directed it in the right way.

We are talking here about elite sportsmen competing at a very high level. However, there is no doubt in my mind the very same lessons apply to everyday living. This applies back to Mike's chapter on Validation. Everyone has the possibility of becoming who you would like to be, it's just a matter of stepping outside the 'box' you are in and opening your mind to new ideas and behaviour patterns.

Mike's observations

At the core of these three stories lies the significance of having a strong sense of self and how often this inner strength is created through adversity.

Perhaps Todd feared not living up to expectations, not being the great player that his fans and others expected him to be. As Newk said earlier, playing for your country adds an order of magnitude more pressure than playing for yourself. It's on these big occasions that we are more likely to 'choke' under the pressure.

What defines a big occasion? It's any time that we find ourselves well outside our comfort zone, when we are operating in a zone outside what we have learnt to believe about ourselves. For Todd it was the Davis Cup; perhaps for a business professional it might be a major presentation.

There are many examples of choking in elite sport, that great public platform that we all get to observe through our television sets. If you are an Australian golf fan, you would have had the chance to experience a few over the years.

If you consider the MINDsense model, it starts with a sense of self that suggests they are supposed to be successful, or perhaps it starts with a weak sense of self that is concerned with the opinions of others. Why would we be concerned with the opinions of others? It's because we use the opinions of others as a way to self-validate, to prove we are enough. If others like me, then I must be enough. It's the same result we get from being right when we express an opinion. Of course the opinions of others are simply opportunities for those expressing the opinion to be right for their own benefit, which raises an interesting question. Are they expressing an opinion about us for any other reason than self-validating themselves? When you realise this, the opinions of others cease to carry as much weight.

Some people also use results as part of their self-validation. If they succeed or win, it reinforces their sense of self; it proves that they are OK. Remember, we only need to reinforce our sense of self because we now no longer see ourselves as complete, because we now identify ourselves with insecurities and doubts, because we have bought the illusion that we are not enough.

The subconscious contemplation of not meeting these expectations results in an increase in anxiety or fear which in turn leads to a decrease in performance; in other words, a change in behaviour or a stifled execution. As the result gets worse, the anxiety increases and performance drops further. It's the classic choke as emotions impact behaviour in a negative way.

What Newk was able to do with Todd was to stop him thinking about the result and instead focus on breaking serve. When Todd stopped worrying about the result, something he had lost belief in, his anxiety dropped and he got his focus back. With that came the determination to break serve. Newk 'engineered' a change in Todd's emotional state that in turn led to an improvement in performance. Slowly Todd got back on top of his opponent and his belief returned. When you understand the process, you can take the necessary action to turn performance around – Newk the master coach in action.

With Pat Rafter at White City, Newk's approach was remarkably similar. Pat had 'choked' as a consequence of being too focused on the outcome or too focused on not being 'enough'. Newk changed the focus from winning to a 'war of attrition', a real dogfight. Pat was now more focused on the fight than the result, on the fight for each and every point. He was now so much more in the present moment and not too far ahead of himself as you are when you are focused on some future-based result.

What I love most about that story, and I was there that day to experience every point of the epic struggle, was that Pat walked off court that day as a hero – a humble Aussie who had overcome adversity, who had faced his inner demons and triumphed. He walked off court to the applause of a crowd expressing their complete and total belief in his ability to be the best. Eight months later he paid back that belief when he held the US Open trophy. Not only did we believe, but Pat also learnt to believe.

In the epic struggle in Spain, Newk again showed the importance of self-belief and his mastery as a coach in instilling it in his players. He was able to get Lleyton to switch his focus from the match and his ability to last the distance. Rather than getting too far ahead and worrying about his ability to last, or the outcome that was some time away in the future, he was able to bring his focus back to one game at a time.

At each change of ends, Newk was able to get Lleyton to reconnect with his inner sense of self and belief. As they moved through the match, Newk was able to get Lleyton to keep topping it up, to keep believing in each small step.

I have had the opportunity over the years to interview people who have climbed Everest and their approach and messages are remarkably similar. Stand at the bottom and look to the summit and you will be overcome by the immense size of the challenge, a wonderful opportunity for self-doubt to surface: 'Am I enough to achieve this?'

Recognise that the journey starts with one step and commit yourself to making each step the best step that you can and before you know it you are at the summit. Results are a consequence of action; it's time to focus on improving your actions and let the results take care of themselves.

Chapter 7

Awareness and Management of Our Emotional States

Mike

If we contemplate the MINDsense model again we can see that the results we achieve in life are a consequence of the behaviours we engage in or the actions that we take. These behaviours and actions are in turn influenced by the emotional states that we experience throughout life.

Many people today are aware of the importance of focusing on their actions and behaviours, seeking constantly to improve their processes and explore ways to increase the volume and intensity of their activity. Sporting legends like Newk know that if you constantly seek to improve your skills the results will look after themselves. The players who consistently execute their shots better than their opponents, who seek continually to improve their physical and mental fitness, will give themselves the opportunity to collect the most titles.

What is also part of the success formula for many of the world's happiest and most contented achievers is a consciousness about the emotional states that they choose to spend their time in. They realise the importance of their emotional state in the process of accessing the most appropriate behaviour or performance.

One of Australia's funniest people, comedian Anh

Do, is a good mate I have enjoyed working with over the years. He has shared his insights and wisdom with many of the executive teams I have worked with and they have all admired his thoughtfulness and positive approach to life. His best-selling book, *The Happiest Refugee*, should be in everybody's book collection. Anh's greeting to me every time we chat has been unchanged for many years: 'How good is life, Mike?' A simple, positive, happy and appreciative focus on what is good about life. But then, Anh sees himself as a happy, positive person; that is who he chooses to be.

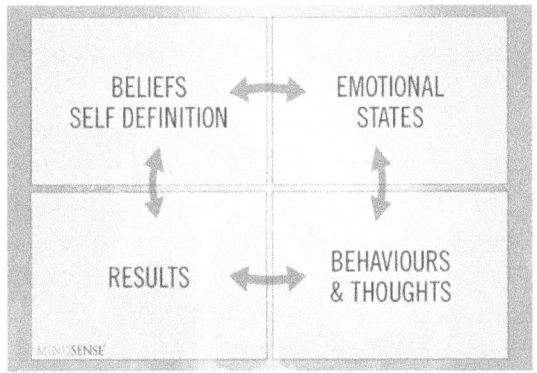

On the flip side, if you are in a negative emotional state you will find it more difficult to access the most appropriate behaviours and you won't think particularly clearly. Anxiety, for instance, is an inhibitor of appropriate action. People feeling anxious are often paralysed and incapable of freely expressing their talents and skills. If you are feeling resigned about your circumstances you are also less likely to engage in action of any sort.

Consider the impact of the following negative emotions on how you might behave:

Anxious	Frustrated	Trapped
Fearful	Angry	Stressed
Doubtful	Resigned	Sad
Worried	Cynical	Bored
Resentful	Depressed	Distrusting
Apathetic	Lonely	Unlucky

Given how important our emotional states are in supporting our actions, we should perhaps give more conscious consideration to them. First of all, we need to take ownership of these emotions.

One of the major differences between people who are happily achieving and the rest of mankind is the ownership that they take of their emotional state, of their feelings. They understand that emotions are felt within our own bodies and are created from within, not placed there by some external force.

Someone in your life could be completely rude and obnoxious towards you for a period of time and how you feel as a result of that is, believe it or not, completely in your hands. In other words, others can't make you angry or upset or frustrated. They are simply not that powerful! This emotion is being experienced within your physiology and as such was created within you.

Of course, if you haven't engaged your conscious mind, in other words you're not stopping to think, your subconscious will deliver the anger or frustration seemingly automatically as part of its ongoing desire for self-validation. In your anger or frustration, you are being right in your view about the other person's beliefs, attitudes or behaviour. Engage your conscious mind, however, and it is completely your choice.

This is a huge revelation for some people. No one can actually make you angry or frustrated or stressed. They can't get into your physiology and alter your emotional state. No one has ever had that ability. It is entirely your choice, though only if you have the consciousness to exercise it. Yes, people can behave in an offensive manner around or towards you, but it is completely your choice how you respond to that behaviour.

Perhaps it is not the events of life that are so important but how we choose to respond to them. Take ownership of how you feel and make the right choices and your world will change in a most profound way. It will change because you will engage in more appropriate behaviour more often, which will give you a greater chance of getting the results that you want more often.

Why should managing how you feel, your emotional state, really matter?

Consider the last time you found yourself anxious or frustrated in dealing with a matter with someone. After the dust settled, perhaps an hour or so later, you probably thought of all the things that you should have said, all the counter-arguments. You also know that you probably didn't put your case forward very well. You were too flustered and struggled to get your point across.

The reason why this is important is that when we find ourselves in a negative emotional state we lose access to clarity of mind. This means we can't access the most appropriate behaviour or thoughts and our ability to produce the result we want is severely compromised.

Quite simply, when you are in a crappy emotional state the most significant sufferer as a result of that state is you! Our emotional state is entirely our choice, although most people rarely exercise that choice. How often do we hear people (including ourselves) say that somebody made me angry or somebody upset me? The reality is that it just isn't true. We find ourselves in this emotional state as a result of our reaction to somebody else's behaviour. Our subconscious mind is running the show, operating the mindspace and the emotion will feel as if it just turned up. But why do we react this way?

If you decide to do one thing today and one thing only, decide never ever again to blame anybody else for how you feel. If you own your feelings, then you are in control of them. If you don't have control over them, how you feel will essentially be in someone else's hands. How you react will also seem to be outside your control and therefore your actions may not be the most appropriate or effective. The end result is that you will feel like you are being 'pushed around' by life.

Think about it for a moment. Who pays the biggest price when we experience the emotions of frustration, anger and anxiety? We do, of course! Prolonged or frequent time spent in these emotions, particularly if we feel them intensely, is harmful to our health. They don't help us; they simply slow us down as we lose effectiveness.

Here's an exercise to restore your conscious mind.

Next time you feel anxiety, stress, anger, frustration or doubt, stop whatever you are doing and focus on identifying the thought or action that delivered the emotional state. Write down the emotional state and the thought or concept that caused it. This will turn off the subconscious and make you consciously aware. Now make a choice: do you want to feel this way?

As an example, if you are cut off in traffic, instead of just getting frustrated stop and write it down. This will help you to stop and think about it. Now make a choice: do you want to feel frustrated? Do you think the other drivers are behaving that way to upset you? Perhaps it would be more accurate to say that they are not thinking about you at all.

Now let's look at three negative emotional states that hinder good behaviours and prevent us from operating at our best: anger, frustration and anxiety.

When we explore these emotions and the reason why we experience them we will soon see that while we may feel them in the present moment we are in fact contemplating different time frames in the process. There are three time frames in life: the past, the present and the future.

Frustration and anger

If you contemplate frustration for a moment, you will recognise that while you may be feeling it in the present moment you have in fact considered a past event in the process. You'll be expressing frustration at something that has already occurred, an event or situation that is in the past. Perhaps you are feeling frustrated because the report you asked for is late and you have a tight deadline. You may be feeling frustrated by the slow driver in front, or perhaps you are frustrated with yourself for missing out on your weekly targets, or the poor shot you hit on the golf course. All of these are the contemplation of a past event, regardless of how recent it may be.

If we contemplate anger, we will recognise that we are also considering a past event. We are angry with something that has already occurred. We disagree with what that person just said, or we feel angry when we see whales being slaughtered, or when we feel someone's behaviour is reckless and stupid.

At the core of these two emotions – anger and frustration – lies judgement. We are making a judgement about past actions (or inactions), judging a situation or a circumstance that has recently occurred. Our focus is on some past event.

Now ask yourself this: has any past event ever changed as a result of your judgement of it? Have you been able to turn back time as you judged this past event and changed the outcome? Of course not. You may subsequently have taken action to prevent the situation occurring again, but your judgement alone achieves nothing. Has your expression of frustration or anger ever changed a past event? Of course not. Subsequent action may change things for the future, but on its own frustration or anger won't.

The emotional state that I have found used as a catalyst for change by many high achievers is the emotion of dissatisfaction. Perhaps the difference between frustration and dissatisfaction is the external manifestation of the emotion and the lack of judgement. Dissatisfaction is best described as the non-judgemental acceptance and understanding of our situation or circumstances and the calm, reflective desire to change it. It is not right or wrong, it just is, but we desire something else. There is no need to judge what is; instead we seek to understand why it is and then create change. We will explore dissatisfaction, the catalyst for change, in the next chapter.

So what is achieved by these negative emotions, frustration and anger? We often link them to subsequent action and describe these emotions as the catalyst for change, though if you stopped to consciously contemplate this you would see that you could take the necessary action without having to feel the frustration or anger. You will note from the MINDsense model that emotions and behaviours are separate aspects of the human condition. Without frustration and anger you may find your responsive behaviours, actions and thoughts a little more effective.

Action, not emotion, creates results. Negative emotional states often slow us down and cloud our thinking. They aren't actually necessary to create change. Why then do we experience these two emotions?

Frustration and anger, the emotions of judgement, are simply part of the subconscious mind's process of self-validation. They are the emotions of self-validation. In the moment that I judge something I am simply being right: 'The report is late', 'The driver in front is too slow.' This self-righteousness momentarily reinforces that I am enough. Note that we don't sit there and think of the need to judge something, we just find ourselves in judgement. The subconscious mind is delivering the thoughts as part of its ongoing self-validation agenda.

Notice that your judgement of the late report does not alter the fact that it's late; nor does your judgement of the driver in front make him speed up. You simply get to be right about the situation. This is all that is achieved. You are momentarily validated as enough.

It serves us no purpose to sit in judgement of this situation, either. If you were to be judging the fact that others are judgemental you would simply be playing the same self-validating game. We would be better served by recognising that life just is and by seeking to understand what is behind these situations, what the cause is of these outcomes.

If you consider the MINDsense model, you will see that we are quick to judge the behaviours of others when we would be better served understanding their beliefs and self-definition that are the cause of their behaviours.

From time to time we come across people who seem to live their lives completely in the past, constantly engaged in complaint about things that have already occurred or in judgement of people's past actions or decisions. We have come to label these people as victims – people who are always right about what has been but who are nonetheless stuck in the misery of all that is wrong in their world. The vast majority of people I encounter who are in this space have grown up in a world full of judgement and opinions. As a consequence, they have turned this judgement back on themselves and constantly question and doubt whether they are OK, whether they are enough.

The result is that their subconscious mind has taken over with its constant need to be right and to prove they are enough. They become like mind junkies. Their self-righteous hits are short-lived; they come back to the reality of self-doubt and insecurity about their enough-ness and then need to find something else to be right about to restore the short-lived balance. It's a vicious mind trap.

Perhaps more damaging, though, is the process of self-judgement, the critical reflection of our own endeavours, thoughts or outcomes. Think about self-criticism for a moment. In that moment we are simply being right about our inabilities or shortcomings or failings. This process does not help us move forward, it simply serves to reinforce the subconsciously held view that we are not good enough, that we are not capable. It is the subconscious mind reinforcing the insecurities, inadequacies, lack of belief that are all part of our view of ourselves, part of our self-definition. The reason it does this is to maintain our predictability, to ensure that we stay true to the subconscious sense of self that our life experiences have created for us and stay in the familiar surroundings that our life has become. This process does not support the notion that we 'can', it reinforces the perception that we 'can't'.

As Newk has mentioned several times, he would venture into the past to analyse his performance, to look for lessons so he could improve and move forward. He would not go into the past to find criticism or fault with himself. He would look for ways to improve.

I've found this trait with many of the world's best whom I've had the pleasure to meet. They protect the strong sense of self that they have of themselves and do not damage it in any way. They know that at their core they are enough and that this is one of their greatest assets and must be protected. There is always an opportunity to improve if they seek to learn and they are enough to be free to explore this without distraction.

The approach that world Ironman champion and one of Australia's fittest ever athletes, Guy Leech, takes to life is a great example of this. He has been a great mate for a decade or more and I have learnt much from him and the way he protects his very strong sense of himself. Everything that Guy takes on in life is successful, and I mean everything. His self-view is clear and strong and he has no doubt that he is more than enough, that if he puts his mind to anything he will succeed. Any hiccups along the way will simply reflect that his actions or approach may not be enough; however they will never reflect that he is less than enough. This separation of self and actions ensures that he never attacks his own sense of self.

We must learn to be kinder to ourselves. None of us ever consciously set out to make bad decisions or sabotage ourselves. We simply make the best decision we can at the time based on the knowledge we have of our circumstances and how we're feeling at the time. Isn't it interesting, then, to observe how often people beat themselves up about the 'mistakes' they have made when they set out in the first place to make the best decision they could. Beating yourself up about past decisions is the subconscious mind's way of reinforcing the underlying sense of self that has question marks and doubt about whether we are enough. Let it go.

Sure, I've made decisions that I'd now make differently if I had my time again, but the reason I would make a different decision now is not because I was an idiot but because new information has come to hand that would influence my decision-making in a different way. I have learnt to look for lessons, not self-validation at my own expense. Not being right that I was wrong. Not being right that I was not enough.

Anxiety

Having explored frustration and anger, let's consider anxiety. The emotion of anxiety or worry is essentially a variation of fear and while we feel it in the present moment you will recognise that we experience it when we project ourselves into the future.

We may feel anxious when we contemplate the targets we are expected to achieve, or are due to present a report to a group of senior executives. Whenever we stretch ourselves beyond our comfort zone – beyond box one of the MINDsense model (our beliefs about ourselves, our sense of ourselves) – we will find ourselves anxious. We are in uncharted territory.

So why are we anxious about these things when it is very clear that none will actually threaten our very existence? We understand the concept of fight or flight, of how the body produces adrenalin to sharpen up our neurological and physiological resources to best prepare us to deal with impending danger. But very few of the things that cause anxiety in life today are life-threatening, so why do we feel anxious?

What accompanies anxiety is self-doubt. The two go hand in hand. If you had complete belief in yourself and your ability to deal with whatever challenges life threw at you, would you ever feel anxious? So, what is the opposite of complete self-belief? Self-doubt. With complete self-belief, we would never experience anxiety so there must be an element of self-doubt in our anxiety.

To understand this further we need to go back to our toddler state. At that age we see the world as it is without judgement. It just *is*. We're introduced to the concept of judgement by others as they validate themselves as enough by being right about whatever it is that they are judging. We're not equipped at that young age to be able to process that effectively and it leaves us now questioning things in life that we had never questioned before. We are now not so sure whether what once just *was* is good or bad, beautiful or ugly. We become uncertain when once we were certain.

Significantly, where we were once enough, we are now not so sure. Each time we were the subject of judgement we experienced hurt as we found ourselves being put down. Someone else's negative opinion of us, their assertion that we were less than enough, brought with it a sense of loss and a sense of pain.

As part of the subconscious mind's job of managing our survival, it seeks to steer us away from things in life that threaten our existence or that question whether we are enough. It steers us by delivering emotional states that stop us in our tracks or slow us down – emotions like fear and anxiety. As the

MINDsense model highlights, emotional states affect behaviour. Fear often paralyses, stopping all action, while anxiety causes hesitation and slows us down.

If we have grown up in an environment of judgement, and to some extent this is true for all of us, we'll find ourselves uncertain whether we are enough and we may have a painful subconscious association with judgement as a consequence of being judged and put down. When we feel that we may be judged, we feel anxious. The subconscious mind seeks to avoid situations where judgement (pain) may occur, so we find ourselves feeling anxious and as a result we retreat or we avoid, as much as we can, putting ourselves in these situations.

If you often feel anxious, you will probably find that your subconscious mind is seeking to avoid the pain associated with being judged. The anxiety will stop you from trying and therefore if you don't try you can't be judged. Problem solved! We avoid situations where we may be judged and this avoidance is driven by the anxiety we are feeling as we contemplate the activity. Anxiety stops us in our tracks. Why do you feel anxious about having to speak in public?

If we want to continue to grow in life and experience much of what life has to offer, we need to explore life and try new and exciting things. In order to explore and try new things, we need to venture outside our comfort zone. We need to learn to believe new things about ourselves and our circumstances. We need to step out from behind the prison bars of our self-definition and evolve to become who we need to be and want to be in life. If we are worried about what others might think of us and the pain associated with their opinions and judgement, we're unlikely to explore life and we'll find ourselves essentially living a prison term that lasts for life.

Anxiety as an emotion is the mind and body's way of avoiding painful situations, like judgement. It's also the emotion we will feel whenever we step outside our comfort zone, beyond what it is that we have learnt to believe about ourselves. Beyond who it is that we think we are. This self-view has been created by the events of our life and our subconscious mind seeks to lock it in to ensure our prolonged predictability. It doesn't want us venturing into new territory. It uses anxiety to get us to hesitate, to slow us down and step away from growth and change.

Several years ago I decided that I wanted to pursue a childhood desire and learn to play the guitar. I bought a beautiful electric guitar on eBay from Chris, a local guy who was himself a very accomplished musician. After a few weeks of unsuccessfully looking for a guitar teacher I felt would be a good fit for me, I approached Chris and asked him if he was interested in becoming my guitar teacher.

Three years of occasional lessons and playing passed when one night Chris suggested that I was ready to join him and play at one of his favourite 'open mic' nights at a Sydney café. At the suggestion of playing live, my anxiety level jumped and my subconscious mind immediately looked for ways to avoid the situation.

The problem for my subconscious mind was that I knew what was going on. It didn't want me to change. It didn't want me to grow and become someone different to the view it had of me. It didn't want me to put myself in a place where my efforts might be judged. While it was a few weeks before I was able to join Chris, the day arrived and my anxiety was with me at some level all day. By agreeing to play live I was challenging myself and what it was I believed about myself. I was on the edge of growth. I knew the experience wouldn't kill me and I consciously challenged my subconscious mind every time the anxiety levels jumped and self-doubt surfaced.

Later that night I stepped off the stage firmly believing something new about myself. My family may think I am deluded in my belief in my guitar playing, but there are now more things I can do in life as a consequence of having the consciousness to navigate my way through the anxiety. I had grown and I will continue to grow in life.

We need to recognise that whenever we are presented with opportunities to grow in life the experience will be accompanied by anxiety. I've learnt to see the anxiety as the sign of a growth opportunity – not to be feared but simply recognised for what it is. I want to continue to grow and experience more of my true potential in life, not shying away from living my best life. I understand anxiety and with consciousness I can process it and step beyond it.

Positive emotional states

Finally, now that you understand the negative emotional states, let us explore the positive emotional states and how we could better manage them.

As we explore positive emotional states we recognise that they support a wider range of behaviours and actions. We have more options at our disposal. Different positive emotional states also support different behaviours. How would someone who was feeling curious behave? They would ask questions and listen. How would someone who was feeling tenacious behave? They wouldn't give in easily.

Consider the impact of the following positive emotions on how you might behave:

Courageous	Relaxed	Generous
Certain	Calm	Interested
Curious	Sharp	Wise
Creative	Strong	Fearless
Free	Warm	Selfless
Confident	Intense	Spontaneous
Happy	Trusting	Loving
Excited	Fun	Fulfilled
Passionate	Engaged	Healthy
Energised	Powerful	Peaceful
Exhilarated	Patient	Sexy
Proud	Motivated	Lucky
Humble	Grateful	Purposeful
Tenacious	Resilient	Focused

As you contemplate the MINDsense model for a moment and think about the result or outcome you want, the next step will be to identify the action you need to take to produce this result. What behaviours do I need to engage in? As we move back through the model we then need to contemplate what emotional states will support those actions.

Have you ever stopped to think about the importance of your emotional state in giving you access to the most appropriate behaviours? Those at the top of their game, the content, happy achievers in life, understand the importance of emotional states and have learnt to manage them as they seek to achieve what they want.

Football teams gee themselves up before they run onto the field; rock bands psych themselves up before a performance; tennis stars think about their state before they walk onto Centre Court. All of these are examples of getting access to the right emotional state so that you can engage the most appropriate behaviour.

I once heard this concept referred to as an emotional cocktail – the process of choosing three or four emotional states that in combination would support your desired actions and endeavours.

Imagine how Newk would have played if he walked out onto Centre Court at Wimbledon feeling resigned, anxious and angry. How difficult would it be to play well and give yourself a chance to win in that state? What if he walked onto Centre Court feeling strong, confident, determined and tenacious? This is a choice the best in the world consciously stop to make before they 'perform'.

When you walk in the door at home each night to your family, what do they get if you are feeling tired, annoyed and stressed? How do you behave? What about if you took a few moments and decided to be loving, excited and curious?

When you have a colleague who is struggling at work, what works best – frustrated, apathetic and trapped or compassionate, curious and enthusiastic?

We have a choice here to decide what emotional

state we want to be in to give ourselves the best chance of experiencing the outcomes we desire. With consciousness we get to make this choice whenever we want and the more we exercise this conscious choice the greater the chance we give ourselves of getting what we want from life.

A redefining process

This conscious selection of our emotional state is an incredibly powerful tool to have in life. From the MINDsense model you will recognise that we are consciously managing box two, our emotional state, and through that ensuring we access the most appropriate behaviours and giving ourselves the best chance to get our desired result.

Through the conscious selection of our emotional state we are also consciously defining ourselves for that moment. 'Right now I choose to be ...' We step past the self-definition that life has created for us and instead consciously replace it with a definition of our choosing, one that supports us in that current moment.

If your view of your self – your belief about who you are – doesn't support what you would like to achieve or experience, how do you move forward? What if instead of accepting your subconscious view of yourself you explored who you would need to be to engage in the required actions to achieve what you wanted?

As you look over the list of positive emotional states above you will recognise that you have experienced every one of them at some point in your life. These states do not come to you from some external source; they are all in you already. We simply need to invoke them consciously as required. If you want to experience the complete freedom in life that the fearless two-year-old knows and that you have forgotten, you simply need to let go of the self-definition that life has created and go back to being undefined like the two-year-old, an empty vessel. Then instead of having a self-definition that acts as a prison cell you attempt to drag around for life, simply choose your emotional cocktail and define yourself for the moment. Instead of a life-created self-definition that may not support where you want to go in life or what you want to experience, you consciously replace it with one that does. Then when that moment has passed let the cocktail go and be ready to create the next one for when you need it.

These emotional cocktails are like affirmations or mantras. A client once told me that he thought choosing and reciting an appropriate positive mantra seemed a 'bit weird'. That was until I told him that his subconscious mind had been engaged in affirmations and reciting mantras all of his life. The affirmation or mantra that reinforced his self-view with all of its doubts and uncertainties. It was now time to start positive, consciously chosen affirmations to replace the limiting, subconscious ones.

When I took this on for myself I chose ten words to define myself. I was clear from the outset that this is my life and it is my choice. If you would like to express a judgemental opinion about my ten words, be my guest. Your opinion will be part of your own self-validation. Your own chance to be right.

My ten words were, Strong, Determined, Capable,

Successful, Disciplined, Tenacious, Resilient, Kind, Caring and Generous. Why did I choose these words? Because I can. In the time it took me to choose these words I went from being uncertain about who I was to very certain about who I was. My ten words were also unquestionably enough.

The end result is that you then have the freedom to be a true chameleon, free to move through life being whoever you want to be.

Now what's possible?

Newk's response

As a teenager growing up I was always interested in what my mind was capable of achieving, or in some cases causing my physical body not to achieve. I became aware through experience that positive anger helped me, negative anger hurt me, frustration only hurt and invited negativity, and anxiety caused bad performance and unhappiness. The question was to try and understand how, why and when those various emotions (or forces) were making their move to enter my mind and body.

As we have worked our way through this book I get the feeling Mike smiles to himself every time I refer to these forces as if they are almost like people and you can reach out and touch them. This is simply my layman's way of identifying them and when I do talk to kids, and sometimes adults, I can sense they understand the simplicity of expression and therefore can identify more easily with what may happen to them.

At 18, I was contacted by a guy who said he had been watching my matches, was involved in psychology and felt he could help me. After talking to my parents, I said OK let's give it a try. Remember this was back in the early 1960s and sports psychology was in its infancy.

Over a three-month period I finished up spending about 18 hours with the gentleman and it had a very profound effect in the furthering of my knowledge of myself and how to deal with all the situations I would have to confront if I were to become the best tennis player I could be. After the time I spent with the psychologist, I didn't go back again because I felt I had gained some very positive insight into ways to improve myself and now it was up to me to put all of this into practice.

I won't go into all of the things we did but there were a couple of interesting ones. If I had to play Centre Court (or some other court) Wimbledon, the day before I would stand at the back of the court, close my eyes and imagine I was embracing the whole court in my arms. The next day when I walked out for my match it would feel like I was coming home. I also developed a technique a few years later of walking through in my mind the beginning of a match about an hour before we were to commence play.

I would recommend this for anyone about to make a speech or attend an important meeting where they have to make a presentation. Occasionally at Wimbledon the dressing room would be full and quite noisy, so I would lock myself in one of the toilets, close my eyes and go through the routine.

Worrying about winning or losing can bring on anxiety, fear and negativity, so over the years I trained myself to adopt an attitude before and during a match that said very clearly, 'You have done everything you can to prepare mentally and physically; your job now is to give it 100 per cent. If you are good enough you will win, if not it simply means your opponent was better on the day.' With this attitude, I took away the fears of winning and losing; it was simply a matter of giving it 100 per cent, a situation I relished.

It's a pretty simple equation if you think of Kipling's quote about dealing with Triumph and Disaster: the fact is there will be a winner and a loser, so put all your energy into performing at your best, and in that way you can walk away with your head held high, proud of yourself, no matter the outcome.

Mike's observations

I have already mentioned my desire to keep the MINDsense journey simple. This is not to diminish the complexities of the mind but to make it easier to comprehend.

Many people I meet have a vast library of self-help books that promote the self-development journey, yet very few have ever done anything with the messages. Some have intellectualised the content and become subject matter experts, yet their lives have not changed. I think this is often the case because the concepts are presented in an overly technical way.

As I explored the various concepts I was learning I would constantly ask myself, 'How does this feel? How am I experiencing what they are talking about? How does this manifest itself in my life?' I explored anxiety and how I experienced it. I was keen to think my way through the sequence of events that surrounded my feelings and to put a simple view of it forward. If we make it too technical, we just give the sub-conscious mind a great excuse to continue resisting change.

What I like about Newk's response is that he talks about his layman's approach to treating the negative emotions he experienced from time to time as people, in other words external forces. I am sure that some academics may view this as naive or overly simplistic, but let's remind ourselves who the world champion was, who was number one in the world. Call his ap-proach what you like, but you can't argue with its effectiveness.

Newk was learning how to think well from an early age. His time as an 18-year-old with the psychologist introduced him to the concept of visualisation, experi-encing something first in your mind so that your mind has a chance to process the circumstances before you actually have to go through the experience. It's a great preparation to think your way through an event so that there are no surprises, if any, when the 'live' time comes along.

This process would leave Newk with positive feel-ings about what he was about to embark on. By spending time in the stands looking over the court on the eve of a big match he was associating with good feelings about his upcoming match. This was his court, he was strong, ready and confident. In his own way he was practising his emotional cocktail. He was connecting with who he wanted to be, the most ap-propriate sense of self if he was to get the job done.

Finally, while he clearly desired a successful result, what was more important was giving it his best. The result wasn't all-important. It was not required for him to prove that he was enough, because his sense of self was already strong. He was now free to go on court with a clear mind, free of the anxiety associated with failure. Being there was enough; now what to do with this opportunity?

Chapter 8

Dissatisfaction – the Precursor to Change

Mike

When we venture out into the big wide world from our childhood home we leave with a view of what we have come to think is possible for us in life and how we think and perhaps expect life to go for us. Along the way we go through periods of growth and development as we learn new things about ourselves and expand our beliefs about ourselves. Life is both exciting and challenging but we feel equipped to keep moving forward. Our world is opening up in front of us and we are able to expand with it.

Then something happens and we find the pace of change slowing down. We are now more challenged than excited. We get the sense that we have plateaued out or stalled. We may get stuck for a period of time before something changes and we get moving again, heading forward in life on a path of growth and expansion. Unfortunately, for most people the plateaus last for a long period of time, sometimes for a lifetime.

Perhaps the answer to leading a rich and fulfilled life is in minimising the amount of time we spend on the plateaus. How do we continue to improve and grow and stay in that zone where life is exciting and rewarding and very stimulating, where we are moving forward and learning?

In order to continue growing and expanding with

life we need to continually evolve what it is that we believe about ourselves. Think box one of the MINDsense model. Therefore, if we have plateaued or stalled we recognise that we have in fact stopped growing. We are not learning to believe anything new. Perhaps instead of learning to believe something new to continue growing, we shift to being right about our current beliefs. We become resigned to our supposed fate, self-validating at our own expense.

At the point when people start to move forward again, a performance breakthrough takes place. They simply start to believe in something new and this in turn supports a new behaviour. Think back to our MINDsense model; if we are to produce a different result (get off the plateau), then we must start to behave differently, which requires us to believe something new.

In earlier discussions we talked about our subconscious and how it creates a self-definition of us based on our life experiences. As we experience life our subconscious develops a view of the world and how we exist in it. It builds a framework for us and decides who we are in it, our self-definition. The primary function of your subconscious mind is to keep you alive and to do this it seeks to create a level of certainty, to know where everything in our world belongs and who we are relative to the world in which we operate. In its desire for a world of certainty, our subconscious mind then seeks to lock us into this self-definition to maintain this status quo and our predictability.

Our plateaus in life are essentially nothing more than situations where our circumstances in life and the limitations in our self-definition are aligned. We may desire more but we don't believe we can have more. We are that self-fulfilling prophecy of self. In this place we find ourselves trapped or stuck. Unless we consciously challenge these beliefs and this sense of ourselves, we will remain stuck because we won't learn to believe anything new.

As an example, consider someone who defines themselves as: 'I don't have much willpower; I can't stay focused for long'.

Subconsciously they may question their self-worth or have a level of self-doubt as a result of childhood experiences (being bullied or put down) that they have long since forgotten. Let's say that their plateau relates to weight and the fact that their health is in danger.

Now go back and reread their self-definition. Not only has their self-definition led them to this plateau as it has underpinned their behaviour to date, but now it is holding them there. All is in order and the mind has certainty. We are fulfilling our destiny, our self-definition. We are right about who we are. As we know, our self-definition is completely self-fulfilling. Game, set and match.

Around us though is a world full of influences that lead us to desire certain things – perhaps to be thinner or healthier or more confident or not to feel self-conscious. As a result of these desires and external influences we may start to question the plateau we are on and the results we are getting or the way we are experiencing life. We start to feel dissatisfied because we actually desire something different from what we are experiencing. It's what you do with that dissatisfaction that matters, how we process this dissatisfaction. This dissatisfaction is the starting point in our journey to get off the plateau.

At this point remember we are fighting our subconscious and its desire to maintain our predictability and certainty by locking us into our self-definition. It wants to maintain the status quo by keeping us on the plateau. It wants us to continue believing that we lack the willpower and the focus. As dissatisfaction is the key to getting off life's plateaus and growing, our subconscious seeks to diminish or suppress our dissatisfaction in order to keep us on the plateau. To do this, it often resorts to either hope or denial.

Hope

How often have you looked at a situation in your life where things are not going to plan and hoped that things would improve?

'I hope those three deals come off this month so that I make my numbers.'

'I hope they don't find out what happened.'

'I hope my health holds out despite my weight and I get to live a long life.'

'I hope I am one of the few that smoking doesn't kill.'

When we start to hope that the result will come out OK, we usually stop doing the very things that will help us get the result. Hope replaces behaviour or action. When we hope it is as if we throw all of our balls up in the air and hope that the gods catch them, rearrange them and send them back in the right order to give us the desired outcome. Occasionally we will get lucky in life and despite our inaction get a fa-vourable result and this leads us to believe that hope actually works. We need to understand that when we start hoping we are in danger, because we will stop taking the very action we need to take to get the res-ult we want.

Hope defers or diminishes dissatisfaction and simply leads to us spending more time on the plateau and therefore more time resigned to our circum-stances. It slows us down.

Denial

How often do we look at a situation in our life and tell ourselves that things are not really as bad as they seem? Notice in these situations what we are being right about:

'I am only 20 kg overweight; it's not that bad and it could be worse.'

'Eighty per cent of sales budget isn't that bad. I'm not the worst performer.'

'He's only abusive after he's been drinking, not all the time.'

In all of these situations our denial of how things are prevents us from getting sufficiently dissatisfied to take action and we remain stuck on the plateau. We are just deferring the dissatisfaction, putting it off for a later time; but sometimes we don't get the chance to sort it out later. In both hope and denial we have a counter to dissatisfaction and the only person who really loses out is us as we consistently fail to achieve the result that we desire. After being stuck on the plat-eau for some period of time, we will start to feel a

degree of dissatisfaction with our plight and the resignation that comes with it. Dissatisfaction and what we
do with it is the key to getting off life's plateaus. So
how do I drive dissatisfaction so that I spend less time
on these plateaus?

High achievers in today's world drive dissatisfaction, that quiet, reflective desire for something else, by
consistently reviewing both the results they are producing and the emotions they are feeling and then
assessing them against the standards they have set for
themselves and their lives.

'Am I achieving the results that I desire?'

'Am I experiencing life the way that I want to?
Does it feel great?'

Whenever there is a gap between where we are in
life and where we aspire to be in terms of either the
results we are producing or how our life journey feels,
there is the potential for dissatisfaction.

When we raise our standards around our goals and
aspirations higher the gap between where we are and
where we want or desire to be widens and with that
the potential for dissatisfaction increases. This dissatisfaction is very useful; it is the starting point to
us getting off the plateau we are stuck on. The high
achievers I have met in life, like Newk, are very good
at getting dissatisfied; their thought processes generally drive higher levels of dissatisfaction than most
people and hence they keep moving forward. They do
not rest on their laurels. The standards they set for
themselves in life, the goals they aspire to, are high.

The dissatisfaction they feel from time to time
along the way is not an angry, frustrated dissatisfaction, though. It is a quiet, inner reflective dissatisfac-

tion that often comes with a level of excitement as they consider the new possibilities, as they start to see the path. The average human being who is experiencing the frustration of being stuck in a rut (or on a plateau) doesn't understand why their problems don't go away, why they can't move forward. Rather than increasing their dissatisfaction, they inadvertently lessen it and remain stuck.

How do they do that? Well, as they set off in pursuit of their once worthwhile goals they often hit a few snags along the way. As we know, nothing of any real value comes without some sustained effort and these snags are all part of life's test. If you are going to achieve great things, then you need to earn them. Passing the tests is all part of earning the result.

Rather than stand up to the tests with strength, focus, resilience and tenacity as their consciously chosen emotional cocktail in the face of these challenges, their subconscious mind steps in with doubt and they weaken and lower their sights. They now aim to achieve something less than originally planned. And they often keep lowering their sights as they hit each new challenge.

When this happens we stall in life and as a result we often redefine what we believe to be possible for us in life and then lower our sights and expectations. We compromise on our original expectations for life and as a result our performance starts to drop. We end up living out a compromised existence full of frustration and anxiety as we give up on all or some of our dreams.

As we lower our sights, the gap between where we are in life and where we want to be reduces and the potential for dissatisfaction decreases. Particularly important here is that the potential strength of the dissatisfaction weakens. At this point, resignation steps in.

At the point of the test when the challenge to achieving our desired goal arose, our subconscious mind stepped in and reinforced the historical self-view that we couldn't overcome it and that we weren't enough. Rather than consciously challenge this historical view, we unconsciously accepted it and lowered our sights. What accompanies this acceptance of something less is a feeling of disappointment. We're not exactly jumping out of our skin with joy as we settle for less.

The subconscious mind seizes the opportunity and steps in. To accompany the resignation and to justify it we find ourselves subconsciously creating stories and excuses to validate why we can't achieve the outcome.

'I'm not that strong anyway.'

'I don't seem to be able to focus for that long.'

'I wasn't really given the opportunity to make it happen.'

As with all our validations our stories and excuses present another opportunity for us to be right, to reinforce and validate that historical, subconscious sense we have of ourselves. It's another opportunity to prevent us from changing our sense of self, from challenging that predictability that our subconscious mind is so intent on protecting. The subconscious mind wins again.

To move on from our plateau, to start to grow again, we need to learn to believe new things.

Resignation presents as just the opposite. Resignation is the reinforcement and justification of our existing subconsciously held beliefs.

When it comes to dissatisfaction there are two things to understand. The sooner you get dissatisfied the sooner you will resolve the challenge, get off the plateau and start moving forward again. Dissatisfaction is a very useful emotional state. Understand it and use it to your advantage.

Remember, all emotional states turn up for a reason. Dissatisfaction is no different. You now know what it means and what to do with it.

So the big question for you right now is this:

What are the standards by which you are operating your life? What standards have you set for how you want to experience life? Are suffering and frustration part of the deal or have you set your sights on living with peace, calm, strength and power? What standards have you set for your career? Are you working at being the best 'you' that you can be or are you simply making up the numbers and turning up for the pay cheque each week (and running the risk that someday the system will spit you out the back), resigned to the notion that you are not capable?

What standards have you set for yourself as a parent? Are your kids learning how to build the strength of mind necessary to live a fulfilled and loving life in the twenty-first century or are they growing up in an environment like the majority of the human race where constant judgement and the expression of opinions leads to insecurity, self-doubt and the resultant negative behaviours of intolerance and fear are pervading? Do you allow your subconscious mind to continue unchecked with its self-validating noise about enough?

Time to raise your standards and get dissatisfied! As the gap between where you are currently at in life and where you want to be widens, as you raise your standards, your dissatisfaction increases. Now that you are dissatisfied, in the next chapter we'll explore the thought processes you can use to ensure that you consistently get what you want from life.

Newk's response

I hear what you are saying, Mike, and couldn't agree more. Everyone's path along our life journey is different and at various stages it can do nothing but good to re-evaluate where you are and to make sure you haven't compromised on the standards you have set for yourself. Every time I've done this I have experienced that feeling of dissatisfaction which has led to a determination by me for some sort of change.

Personally I've gone through a few of these occasions. One of the most meaningful was in my late forties when I re-evaluated my standing as a dad and thought about the quality of relationship I wanted with my children. My wife and I were married at 20 and 21 and had three children before we were 30 years old. They therefore grew up and travelled the world as I was going through a pretty heady existence at the top of the tennis world and later being involved in business activities around the world.

As they entered adult life, I felt there had to be some issues they might have with our relationship due to me being away from home or being too caught up in my own world. It wasn't that we didn't get on OK, it was mainly a desire I had to try and create a true adult friendship with my kids, and I knew that could not be possible if baggage was around which had not been dealt with.

Of course you love your kids and they love you, but the true test is whether you really like and know each other as real friends do. Parents are voicing disapproval (and approval) at their kids from a young age but kids rarely get the chance to respond and often misunderstandings occur that can be life-defining for our kids. Mike has already talked about this process in great detail.

What I wanted to do was make sure there were no unresolved issues in our relationship. So I sat down with each of them and gave the invitation to voice anything on their minds that had happened over the years which was of concern to them, no matter how small. My job was to sit and listen, not to voice opinions, as this was all about their feelings.

At the end I gave each one the same answer! 'Thanks for sharing those feelings. I acknowledge, accept them and apologise for not performing better at the time. As you know, I was trying to be the best in the world at my profession and in doing so I failed you in the things you have expressed. I can only say how much I love you and I tried my hardest to be the best dad I could under those circumstances.'

Today we have a wonderful relationship based on love of each other, but more importantly in my book we truly like each other. I am as much their friend as I am their father.

As I look back on my life, I see the decade of the

seventies as having been a great challenge for me personally as I fought to be a good son, good husband, father, and the best tennis player I could be.

By the end of 1971, a lot had happened over the preceding two years. My mother travelled with us for four months leading into my end of June Wimbledon campaign – us being my wife Angie and 20-month-old son Clint. Mum had been looking after my ailing father for two years and as she had never been to Wimbledon I thought the trip would do her good. As an extra present, I won the singles and doubles, so as you can imagine she was a pretty proud Mum.

Our second child, Tanya, was born in early June 1971 and four weeks later I won Wimbledon again. As 1972 began I was finding it increasingly difficult to travel and leave Angie taking care of the kids. I was a little torn between my career and my young family.

The 1972 circuit began in mid-February and for six weeks in a row I lost first round to players I had always routinely beaten. For the first time in my life I was suffering from severe dissatisfaction and not sure of what to do about it. To Mike's point about plateaus – I was unclear of the goals I was trying to achieve and of the standards I was setting for myself. I was in a sort of limbo.

It all came to a head in Quebec when I went out to dinner with a few mates after another weak performance. Dinner was followed by quite a few drinks until around 2 a.m. I announced I was going home and quitting tennis.

The result was a huge tongue-lashing from two Aussie mates, Allan Stone and Ray Ruffels, who were also on the circuit, as they accused me of being gutless and a quitter. We had grown up playing tennis together, they respected what I had achieved and couldn't believe I was a quitter. In hindsight I can see that doubt and self-pity and my subconscious mind were gaining strength. I was just ambling along without the direction that I normally had in life.

After they had abused me for 15 minutes I sat quietly for a while and then turned on them saying, 'OK, I'm going to show you bastards, I'm going to win the Las Vegas event in three weeks' time!'

I took off for Charlotte (our next tournament) the next day and began a rigorous training regime, reaching the quarter-finals with a renewed enthusiasm. The next event was Las Vegas and I did win it; in fact I was so determined that after straining a stomach muscle in the semis I had to have a pain-killing injection into the muscle prior to the finals, coming out and playing like a man possessed.

In hindsight I should have given Allan and Ray a percentage of my prize money! What they had done was to shock me out of my self-dissatisfaction and feeling sorry for myself and my life. I was 27 years old, nearing the height of my career, and it would have been ridiculous not to see it out for three more years.

Allan and Ray had essentially told me that the John Newcombe standing in front of them wallowing in doubt and self-pity was not the John Newcombe they knew and this caused me to stop and reconnect with my true sense of self. As I reflected in my mind I knew they were right. I had prided myself on my strength and determination and they helped me to find it again. With that, I was no longer lost.

Mike's observations

I've had the pleasure of observing the Newcombe family at close quarters over the years and John and Angie have a lot to be very proud of in their three children. Being a few years younger, I feel very fortunate to have had Newk as a generous role model for me when I set about being a father to my own two beautiful daughters, Alex and Lucy.

I say generous because he has always been prepared to share his experiences with great honesty and vulnerability and this has made the learning experience so real for me. The standards he set for himself around the quality of relationship he wanted with his kids and the honesty with which he approached it has been inspirational. I know it hasn't always been easy for them, as is the case in all families whether you are famous or not, but the commitment to maintaining a strong level of connection has always appeared unwavering. It has been a great lesson in staying committed to your standards and not compromising.

Newk's experiences in early 1972 and the process of regrouping he undertook demonstrate a number of the MINDsense principles. It would seem his tennis started to struggle as a result of starting the year without any clear goals or objectives. Without any goals, what's the point of being on the circuit? Essentially, Newk was now just making up the numbers. Added to this was a degree of internal conflict as he questioned whether he should be on the circuit or at home with his young family.

As his results suffered, he found himself uncertain about who he was. The old Newk didn't lose six first-round matches; he was focused, determined and successful. The Newk who woke up each day in the early part of 1972 was anybody but that. Probably for the first time in many years Newk was starting to question who he was and he was uncertain of what the answer was. His self-definition was unclear.

You will no doubt recognise that when we are uncertain about our very sense of self, who we are, it is not a pleasant place to be in life. This uncertainty can be stressful; at the very least it is a time of ambivalence when we feel rather lacklustre about life, with no great sense of purpose. I'm sure this was an uncomfortable experience for Newk, who was much more accustomed to being on top of things in life. He would not have enjoyed this experience, which probably had him question even further whether he should still have been out there on the tour. This was what he expressed to Allan and Ray in Quebec.

If we explore this in terms of the MINDsense model, we can see that Newk was unclear about both the result he wanted to achieve and his self-definition. He was aimless and uncertain, a foreign place for the best tennis player in the world!

Neither Allan nor Ray would have been used to hearing such uncertainty and negativity from Newk. They would have known him to be clear and confident in his approach and they weren't about to tolerate anything less from their mate. Their reaction helped Newk to reconnect with his sense of himself. He consciously reminded himself who he was, had chosen to be. He restored the fire in his belly and then re-evaluated his standards. First-round losses were certainly not good enough and he was no longer going to accept them. He didn't stop at getting past the first round, though; he went all the way to declaring his desire to win. He restored his expectations to the highest of standards, winning in Las Vegas. With his standards restored to where they should be, his dissatisfaction kicked in and became the catalyst for the turnaround in his performances.

The end result was that he had congruency with his desired outcome, his belief in himself, his sense of self, and it was all driven by an increase in dissatisfaction that was brought about by raising his standards.

Where could you apply the same process?

Chapter 9

The Power of Belief

Mike

I remember when I was a kid at school how much I looked forward to my favourite subjects and to exploring and absorbing all the new things there were to learn. Like all kids, there was a real sense of achievement as I mastered new concepts and could make sense of something. Then when I was ready to move on my teachers would be there with the next piece of the subject to learn.

In my late thirties I found myself back in this space as I took myself back to school to learn how to build a strong mind. I was excited as I learnt new things; however this time there was no formal teacher, I had to uncover the various aspects of the subject for myself. This probably made the sense of achievement even greater. What I could do, though, was take the things I'd learned and discuss them with various mentors I had – people like Newk who had been or were the very best in the world at what they do.

As I engaged with this process I became aware of a really interesting phenomenon. The answers to the questions I had or the confirmation of the insights I had developed were not difficult to uncover at all. In fact they were all around me and it seemed that rather than me having to find them they would find me.

We often see this more easily when we consider

the challenges other people face. We can see the answers to others' challenges all too easily, yet we often seem blinded to how to solve our own. The subconscious mind is at work seeking to contain us in our predictability by making sure we don't see that which might lead to change. It doesn't matter to our subconscious mind if somebody else evolves and grows as they find answers to life's challenges, as long as we don't change.

What I had done in my own journey was to make building a strong mind really important to me and I wasn't aware at the time of how important that decision was going to be in the learning process. Any time we consciously make a decision that something is important to us, the filters on our mind start to open up and allow us to see information that relates to the matter. If you have a particular hobby, for example collecting stamps, you will be drawn to any information that passes by that relates to the subject. You'll hear references to stamp-collecting on TV when others wouldn't. The word 'stamp' will seemingly jump out of the pages of newspapers and magazines. You'll see it everywhere. Of course those references to stamp-collecting haven't just started to appear in the media, they have always been there. All that has happened is that your mind filters have opened and you have started to see them.

I was discussing this concept with a group one day when one of the team recounted his own experience which provided a wonderful example of this. He was in the market for a new car and finally settled on a BMW and decided on a certain dealership to do the deal with. As he went through the various options, he found himself drawn to a particular shade of green that really appealed, particularly because it was also a colour you had to custom order and was therefore very, very rare. In fact, he had never seen it before on the road. With the deal done, all he had to do was wait for the car to arrive from overseas, a waiting period of six to eight weeks at the time.

No sooner had he walked out of the dealership with the paperwork signed, in fact the very next day, what did he see? The very same, rare-coloured BMW on the road. In fact over the next weeks he counted seven BMWs the same colour. Where had they all come from suddenly? Of course the answer is that they had always been there, he just hadn't seen them before. The answers to our challenges, to all the questions we have or the things we want to learn, are right in front of us. We just need to open up the filters on our minds so that we can see them.

Make building a strong mind important to you and watch what turns up in your life: lots of answers that have always been there just waiting for you to be open to them.

With my desire to build a strong mind firmly focused, I began the journey. I remember at the time being excited but also feeling a little apprehensive. This was the first part of my learning process. I came to realise that the excitement came when I consciously contemplated a new way of experiencing life and the apprehension, or anxiety, came in response from my subconscious mind as it defended my existing state of being and tried to resist the process.

With my new-found consciousness I learnt how powerful choice is, particularly as it related to the

MINDsense model. It meant the ability to consciously choose what to do and what emotional state to be in at any time. I took this up as a sort of contract with life.

There was a time in the past when many communities emerged from winter into the time of new growth that is spring and one of the very first things they would do was stage a festival to honour their gods. In essence they would take something of value to the community, such as a prize calf or lamb, and sacrifice it to the gods. They would offer up something of value to the gods and in return ask them to provide good health, abundant crops and peaceful times.

In this relationship, what I saw was first the gift of something valuable and then the hope for something in return – giving first in order to receive. It occurred to me how much that has changed over the years so that today people aren't prepared to offer anything to life or the universe (or the gods) first, they just expect to receive. So many sit across the table from life and say, 'OK, life, if you give me a good job, plenty of money, health and good relationships and a nice house, then I'll be happy and perhaps even excited and passionate about life.' If life could respond I'm sure it would say, 'You're kidding me, right? Why should I care? What are you prepared to offer me first so that I should care?'

In my own journey I made the conscious decision that I wanted to offer something to life or the universe. The successful people I had met along the way who were enjoying the journey in life and achieving their goals all, without question, presented themselves as happy, excited and passionate people and they had no expectations of life or the universe that this was dependent on. They were giving without expectation and it seemed that the universe was rewarding them.

On the other hand, it seemed to me that most people, myself included at the time, were requesting from life all the things they thought would lead to happiness and were in effect being like two-year-olds throwing a tantrum. They wanted to be happy, excited and possibly passionate but in effect they were saying to the universe that they were not prepared to be that person, to be who they wanted to be, to experience life the way they wanted to, unless life gave them something first. If some stranger said to you, 'I won't be happy unless you give me $20,' you would probably reply, 'Why should I care? It's you who's going to miss out on being happy.'

My choice at that time was to choose to be a happy, enthusiastic, determined, excited and passionate person. It's a choice I make every day simply because I can, because that is how I want to experience life. It's a state of existence I choose for my life each day and that I choose to offer to the universe every day, unconditionally; that is, without any expectation of anything in return. What's been wonderful is that from that time it seems that the universe has continued to give me back so much more.

This process is what I call my 'contract with the universe'.

With my growing consciousness, I then started to explore thought processes. Mankind has spent centuries focused on developing and improving processes in an effort to improve effectiveness and productivity. Corporations spend vast sums of money in pursuit of process improvement. The smartest graduates are hired, process flow diagrams are analysed in great detail and fine-tuned and tweaked. I thought that someone somewhere must have studied effective ways for human beings to think and developed thought processes that improved our chances of creating the outcomes we desired. After all, what value would an improved consciousness be if we then didn't know how to direct that consciousness?

I was excited by this pursuit of what I saw as a real life-changer. What if I could find a way to think about anything I was dealing with in life that greatly improved my chances of success? What if there was in fact a proven process for dealing with the thinking required to maximise our potential for achieving what we wanted – if we could learn to become good conscious thinkers?

I was also keen to explore whether there were any proven processes that helped to awaken consciousness and turn off the defensive ramblings of my subconscious mind. It occurred to me at the time that any process I followed would in itself invoke a higher level of consciousness, because if I was in fact following a process I *must* be doing it consciously.

In a short period of time I had gone from being relatively unaware of how my mind worked, let alone understanding the split roles of my conscious and subconscious minds, to being in a place where I was starting to recognise that I could actually become the master of my thoughts, or at least more in control of them.

What happened next in the process was a great surprise. I found the answer right under my own nose in the form of the MINDsense model. While I was using it as a reference tool to understand the connection between the various elements of our human existence, it turned out to be much more useful and powerful than that. It was in itself a way to think and to approach life.

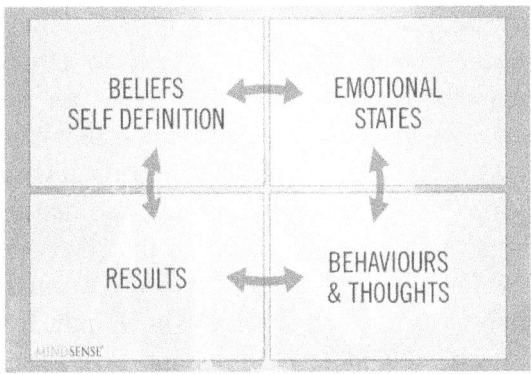

As we have discussed, results are a consequence of behaviours and actions, which are in turn influenced by our emotional state or how we are feeling. Our emotions are in turn a consequence of how our beliefs and self-definition sit with our circumstances.

To that point in time I had been using the model to analyse my reactions to past events. It was essentially a great tool through which to review human behaviour, emotion and the impact of our belief systems.

It then dawned on me that the model was equally as effective in supporting the achievement of desired goals and outcomes, a framework that helped me to project forward into the future with greater congruency in my thoughts, actions and desires. Over the past ten years that I have been using the MINDsense model as a thought process, I can think of very little, if anything, I have wanted that I have not been able to achieve. This is a big statement, I know, but if I haven't achieved my desired outcomes the model will help me understand why and identify what I need to do to get back on track.

Many people I have worked with and mentored over the past decade have been able to achieve the performance breakthroughs they have for so long dreamed of because they learnt how to think through applying the MINDsense process. Significant amounts of weight have been lost by people who had become so resigned to their state of being that they were no longer able to generate any level of dissatisfaction with their predicament. Smokers have quit, Ironman races have been completed and some have even resurrected their careers and started to achieve great results with much less 'effort'. Parents have reconnected with their children and created much stronger and more nurturing environments where their influence on their own kids' self-belief has become more positive.

There has been no greater joy in my career than being able to create these breakthroughs for others.

Here is how simple the process is:

First, we start with box four of the model and identify the outcome or goal (Result) we are trying to achieve. What is the opportunity that is presenting itself that we would like to explore, or the change that we wish to create in our lives? Examples could be as follows:

Losing 20 kilos.

Quitting smoking.

Completing a fun run or perhaps something more challenging like a marathon.

Getting a promotion at work or a transfer interstate or to a new department.

Developing a new skill like public speaking.

Buying a new house or car or taking an overseas holiday.

Buying something new for home or for your favourite pastime.

Now that we have identified what it is that we are trying to achieve, the next step is to identify the action (Behaviour) that we need to take towards the achievement of our goal. What is the first step in the process or what are the things we need to do differently?

We need to identify the steps required. If our goal is to lose weight, the steps could be as follows:

Get up 30 minutes earlier every morning and go for a walk or run.

Prepare your own lunch and cut out snacks at work.

Reduce your meal sizes.

Eat a healthier diet and cut out junk food.

From here we head back to box one and contemplate two questions:

What do I need to believe about myself and my world in order to be able to achieve this?

Who do I need to be in order to achieve this outcome?

Without this conscious process, we are likely to be 'foiled' in our attempts by our subconscious mind as it steps in and rather than explore what is required we will find ourselves contemplating what already is. After all, this is probably what we have done every time we have contemplated achieving our desired outcomes – contemplated our current beliefs and view of ourselves and been right that we 'can't'. This highlights that results are achieved by a process that involves more than developing an action plan. We need to support our plan by making sure our beliefs and our sense of ourselves are aligned with our desired outcome.

Here is an example of this process at work:

A female executive I worked with several years ago finished our year together having achieved all of her work goals and KPIs for the year and had even been acknowledged for her achievements with a CEO Award at the company's annual conference. I asked her how she defined herself as a leader and she said, 'Strong, Determined and Purposeful'. She had been a great student of the MINDsense process and regularly and consciously chose how she was going to define herself. She was exercising her choice as to who she wanted to be and who she needed to be if she was to lead her team well.

When we focused on her goals for the year ahead, there was no mention of work, though. We both knew that her health was an issue and she needed to lose some weight, because she was starting to struggle physically. She had obviously been giving it plenty of thought and had even been given a 'kick up the backside' by her doctor, who advised her that she needed to lose 40 kilograms.

I took a pretty direct line and asked her why she didn't just lose the 40 kilos. What happened over the next ten minutes brought together all the elements of MINDsense that we have discussed so far.

In response to my question, she spent the next five minutes giving me all the reasons why she couldn't lose the weight. 'I'm too busy', 'I don't have time to exercise', 'I'm not disciplined enough', 'It's too late' were just some of the things she said. All of these reasons were simply things that she got to be right about. She didn't feel good about herself with the excess weight and constantly expressed disappointment in herself. One of the few things she got to feel good about was being right about why she couldn't lose the weight. It was a classic case of self-validating at her own expense, of being right about why she couldn't.

At the end of her five minutes of excuses she sat back with a wry smile on her face looking quite pleased with herself, such was the impact of her self-righteousness.

I then asked her what she thought she would need to do to lose the weight and we spent the next couple of minutes considering what she would need to do. The interesting thing was that she knew what was required. She was very clear, because she had heard it all before and it was common sense and she was an intelligent woman. So why didn't she just go out and do it? Quite simply, it was because there was too much oppositional noise going on in her head. She didn't believe she could and besides she was a person with no willpower, discipline or focus. Or at least that's who her subconscious mind had come to see her as and it was intent on making sure she stayed predictably true to that life-created definition.

Having thought through the action plan, I then asked her what she would need to believe to be able to lose the weight. I didn't need to hear or know what she currently believed, with her five minutes of reasons why she couldn't lose the weight. We needed to explore the opposite – what she would need to believe to lose the weight. To create the performance breakthrough and lose the kilos, she needed to learn to believe something new and we needed to identify what that was. We came up with a list of six core beliefs and I asked her to write each one down:

'That I can lose the weight.'

'That I can find 30 minutes every day to go for a walk and get mobile.'

'That I can stop buying junk food and prepare my own lunch.'

'That I can resist snacking during the day.'

'That if I don't the quality of my very existence will suffer.'

'That I need to be a better role model for my kids.'

This was quite a simple list and her challenge now was to stay consciously connected to these new beliefs and to resist the defence of her subconscious mind as it sought to challenge them.

The final question I asked her was who she thought she needed to be if she was to succeed. How did she need to define herself if she was to overcome her weight and achieve her goals? She thought about it for a few seconds and then this smile came across her face as she said, 'I guess I would need to be Strong, Determined and Purposeful.' This was the very definition she had chosen for herself at work. She just needed to apply it to her weight challenge.

With her beliefs and her chosen sense of herself aligned with and supporting the action she needed to take to achieve her goal, she had given herself a chance. When I checked in with her next, some four months later, she had lost 32 kilos, was exercising daily, eating well and feeling really proud of herself. She was enjoying being the 'new, strong, focused, determined and disciplined' person that she had chosen to be and she was living so much more consciously.

This was a person who had battled her weight all of her life and who had developed an array of 'stories' to support why managing her weight was hard – stories that had become real for her but existed only in her head as the defence mechanism of her subconscious mind. Why was it different this time? Why was she able to do all of the things that as an intelligent person she knew she should do? Simply, this time she made sure that her beliefs and her sense of herself, her chosen self-definition, actually supported the outcome she wanted. There was congruency.

The world is full of people who desire change or who wish to create performance breakthroughs in their lives. They know what they want and also what they would need to do to achieve it. It is unfortunately the lack of understanding of their minds that prevents them from turning these dreams and desires into reality. They become their own roadblocks as their subconscious mind dominates the mindspace and protects and defends their existing sense of themselves.

Listen! Your subconscious is probably doing it right now!

Newk's response

My thought process on trying to achieve a desired result on a tough question is to force myself to 'think outside the box'. Obviously, the first thing is that when I force myself to think a certain way I am re-engaging my conscious mind. I am now driving my thoughts. Everyone faces a situation at some time where you appear to have hit a brick wall and things are happening to you and around you that you really don't want to happen.

As Mike talks about above, the key is to stop thinking about the problem itself and focus in on what is the result or outcome you desire. Once you have made that decision, your mind clears itself of previous thoughts, usually negative, and allows you to develop an approach that has a good chance of success.

A prime example is my previous story of the 1970 Wimbledon final against Rosewall, where I was in a winning position and negative thoughts completely disrupted the flow of my mind and body. After leading two sets to one and 3–1, I lost five games in a row to be two sets all, with the crowd and momentum all with Rosewall.

My thought process was to question myself on the result I wanted, and the immediate answer was that I really wanted to win the Championship. It now became apparent that if my current mental attitude continued I had no chance of success, so I decided when I walked out onto the court there would be a tennis ball, a tennis court, and someone on the other side of the net and no other thoughts would enter my mind. I was putting myself into a zone and allowing my conscious mind to do what years of training had developed. The result was a 6–1 fifth set, the best I ever played, and it required a belief in myself to get that result. Any distractions to my thought process and the zone I was in could have been disastrous.

Of course it didn't just happen that I was able to pull myself together at two sets all in a Wimbledon final when I had lost the previous five games, and had worked myself into a negative state of mind wherein my natural instinct of self-belief was being squashed.

I was 26 years of age and as I mentioned earlier in the book my mother had played a strong role from eight years old in helping me to understand myself, especially in how to turn a strong competitive natural instinct into a positive rather than a negative force. The former can be one of your greatest strengths, the latter one of your strongest enemies.

From the age of 12 to 15 I often had very real dreams where I could actually fly like a bird and accomplish amazing things, waking up in the morning feeling very powerful within my inner being, or my soul and mind.

I first travelled overseas in an Australian men's team on a seven-month trip at 17 years of age, playing in Asia, Europe and America. Our manager was Alf Chave, a businessman and keen tennis enthusiast. His bible of life was Dale Carnegie's book, *How to Win Friends and Influence People.*

After a month on tour, Alf gave me a copy to read and over the next two months we had fruitful discussions on Carnegie's thoughts. I really enjoyed the book, although I never became a disciple like Alf. What I did was take all the salient points I believed would help me to become a better and stronger character, and then put them into practice. I can't remember today what they were exactly, but the essence of the book was positive thinking, developing self-belief and ways to discuss sensitive issues with other people to bring about a positive outcome.

In Chapter 7, in my response to Mike's discussion of awareness and management of our emotional states, I talked about how as an 18-year-old I had spent about 18 hours with one of the early sports psychologists and I took away from these sessions more valuable lessons on how to improve my self-knowledge, because only by honestly knowing yourself can you develop great self-belief.

One of the greatest tennis players was Bill Tilden, who ruled in the 1920s and early 1930s. He wrote an excellent book whose original title was *Tennis A-Z* and I found this book to be one of the best I have read. His chapter on 'Match Play and Tennis Psychology' I found fascinating, and in that chapter he talked about how important self-belief is to becoming a champion. He went on to say that you must be careful that extreme self-belief does not become conceit, as conceit is very brittle and can fall into self-doubt under extreme pressure. I took those words to heart.

Another interesting topic was the two ways to break down an opponent's game. The first and obvious one was to attack and wear down the weak areas, which may or may not work as your opponent is probably doing the same to you. The second and more adventurous tactic was to attack and break your opponent's strengths. It's not something they will be expecting and if you succeed you will have shattered their self-belief and therefore their game.

These examples were very important in the early

part of my journey to the top of the tennis world and helped me to stabilise when very serious questions were being asked of me in that Wimbledon final with Ken Rosewall.

Chapter 10

The Benefits of a Quiet Mind

Mike

With all the noise of the subconscious mind filling our mindspace and creating distraction, it's little wonder that many people struggle with their day-to-day lives. The subconscious mind is also the originator of our negative emotional states and these negative emotions are a drain on our energy source.

Let me explain. Imagine you spent the day feeling anxious or angry. What are your energy levels like at the end of that day? These emotional states drain our energy and we often arrive at the end of our day feeling exhausted. Remember, these emotions are delivered by the subconscious mind in its quest for predictability or self-validation.

What if we consciously decided to spend our day happy, motivated and enthusiastic, grateful for what we have in life and the good things we can find in our lives, connected with and conscious of our 'contract with the universe'? At the end of the day we will find our energy levels still high and a bounce in our step.

Have you ever wondered why 'positive', empowered people have so much energy? Why do clinically depressed people spend so much time sleeping or resting? Think emotions and the effect on energy levels. Remember, you can stop and choose your emotional state at any time regardless of your circumstances.

I was once asked by a group of friends to help them learn meditation. They had been off to an introductory class but had struggled to empty their minds of thoughts. They were divided between wanting to 'beat' their plight and being resigned about their prospects. In their introductory class they had spent about 20 minutes relaxing and quietly observing their breathing as they prepared to 'let go' of their thoughts and empty their minds. The letting go of their thoughts was the stumbling block.

When I met with the group several weeks after their introductory class, we talked for 30 minutes or so about the MINDsense model and the separation of the conscious and subconscious minds. It became clear that while they were able initially to consciously stop their thoughts, these promptly came rushing back in, somewhat like the tide. They soon realised that the thoughts that came rushing back in were thoughts of the subconscious mind – random, uninvited and spurious thoughts. As the thoughts came rushing back in, they found themselves consciously aware in one moment of the random thoughts and then caught up in the next moment in the random thoughts themselves. The mind noise just got louder and louder when it was supposed to be getting quieter and quieter.

We explored the very thoughts they experienced at that time and there appeared to be a sequence to their thinking.

First thoughts were an expression of whether they thought they could let go of their thoughts:

'This is going to be difficult.'

'I don't think I'll be able to do this.'

'I've never done anything like this before.'

What do we recognise from these thoughts? They are essentially expressions of doubt in my belief in myself and my ability. They are thoughts that create roadblocks to achieving the desired outcome. They reinforce my negative perception of myself and ultimately discourage change. They say that I 'can't'.

The second series of thoughts were an expression of self-validation, mixed with more self-doubt:

'Why can't I let go of my thoughts? What's wrong with me?'

'I'm hopeless; I knew I wouldn't be able to do this.'

'I bet everyone else can do this but me.'

In these thoughts we see a conversation about whether we are enough. 'What's wrong with me, why aren't I enough?' The second thought is validation that I'm not enough and the third that others are more 'enough' than me.

The group then found themselves in a fight between their conscious and subconscious minds as they first consciously challenged and then submitted to the subconscious mind. This battle created more and more mental noise.

We explored the MINDsense model and the formation of our beliefs and self-definition and the resultant subconscious perception of whether we were enough, then I asked them to let these notions go, to sit for 20 to 30 minutes with 'being enough'. To accept themselves for who they were, the perfect embodiment of a human being, albeit now with a self-view that they were somehow tarnished as a result of the opinions and judgement of others. It was time to wipe the tarnish away. They sat quietly with these thoughts during that time.

One of the group was still struggling after about ten minutes and I could see that she was emotionally on the edge. I got the overwhelming sense that she had never seen herself as enough. She had too easily and too often connected with the fact that she was flawed, in fact seriously flawed, and as uncomfortable as that was she was struggling to let go of that predictable state. As tough a fight as she was having, she desperately wanted to feel 'better'.

We stood in front of a mirror together and I asked her to look closely at herself, to take in the image looking back at her. She broke down and cried. It was just too hard to face herself, as she only saw what was wrong, what was not 'enough'. With coaxing, encouragement and support from me as I reinforced to her that she was more than enough and that all of us there that day could see it even if she couldn't, she started to relax and connect with herself and her reflected image. After a few minutes she was accepting of her own image. Then I asked her to hold out her hands in acceptance and say to herself, 'I am not ten feet tall and bulletproof, I am not perfect, I do not have all the answers, but I am enough. In fact I am more than enough.' She wept again, but this time there was joy in her weeping. After a few minutes, she got her composure back and we rejoined the group, who had remained silently with their own thoughts of being enough.

There was a definite peacefulness with the group and within four or five minutes they were all able to find that meditative state. Each time they moved out of the state, they could find their way back by focusing on their core and allowing themselves to feel the sense of being enough.

The art of meditation has been practised for centuries by people seeking to quieten their minds and find that peaceful place. During my time as an international sporting executive, it was something I was keen to pursue for myself as I attempted to escape the stress and mental noise of corporate life. This was before I learnt that I was the 'cause' of my own noise and stress. I asked my Roshi (Zen master) if he could help, as I was sure he would practise meditation and I was keen to do whatever he did. You could probably imagine my surprise when I asked him what form of meditation he practised and he replied, 'The 24/7 method'.

I learnt that day that while practising meditation is a wonderful, healing and replenishing process it is possible to have a peaceful mind 24 hours a day, seven days a week. We don't have to stop and meditate when we learn to live with the quiet mind that we are seeking through meditation. If you follow the MINDsense principles, the very path of understanding that I took, you too can experience the 24/7 state of a quiet mind.

So much of the noise of the subconscious mind relates to the conversation of whether we are enough. With my meditation group we had simply reconnected with the fact that we were each enough. In fact, to be a human being is to be enough.

When we accept this and allow it to be the truth for us again, we make redundant one of the subconscious mind's most important tasks, that which relates to the ongoing discussion about our enoughness. It is then silenced and peace returns. This enough does not mean we need to stand on top of the tallest building to shout it out to the world. If we felt compelled to do that, it would be because we were still seeking to prove it to others and therefore not truly connected with being enough. No, this is the quiet, calm reflection of our state of completeness. It needs no validation or proof or justification. It just is.

Now imagine if you brought that quiet, peaceful and calm mindspace along with you each day. Your mindspace would be in that state because the subconscious mind had been sidelined, no longer required to validate that you were enough and no longer doubting that you could change and evolve.

In that state you have all of your mindspace available to your conscious mind whenever you need to engage it to solve a challenge or explore possibilities. Often when mentoring executives I have been able to come up with several alternative strategies to help solve a pressing challenge. They often express surprise that I can come up with these ideas when they can't, even though they spend all day with the challenge. The reason is simple. My mindspace is largely free of noise while theirs has been overrun by their subconscious mind and its commentary about their enoughness.

When you allow yourself to reconnect with your true state of being enough and the mindspace quietens, you find your senses are magnified. When you choose to be curious, you explore much more deeply and profoundly; when you are creative, you sail past any boundaries; and when you are tenacious, you endure longer and fight harder than you ever thought you could.

Newk's response

Mike's explanation of the benefits of a quiet mind speaks for itself. As far as I know, nothing of what I have talked about in this book can be achieved without a quiet mind, which can then focus on the job at hand.

Imagine how difficult it would be to play tennis at the highest level if your mind was distracted by other thoughts like being fearful of losing or getting caught up in a bad umpiring decision. These are thoughts that distract you from the most important job you have, to hit the ball with the power and precision that is required to set up the opportunity to win the point.

In Chapter 6, I related three stories from Davis Cup matches where I was captain and was able to assist my players to emerge from positions that looked doubtful at best.

Each of these occasions featured a situation where the player had lost control of his conscious mind and the subconscious had taken over. In Todd's case, he was playing someone he and everyone else knew he should beat and the fear of that not happening had stopped his conscious mind from simply concentrating on competing at his best level, which would be enough to win. My job was to get him to concentrate on one simple goal, which was to break his opponent's serve. Consequently he was able to shut out all the noise, establish a quiet mind which had one objective, the result being that he started playing like the real Todd and won the next three sets.

With Pat Rafter, it was a similar story of interference from the subconscious but for different reasons. Pat did not have fear, he had simply lost self-belief of who he really was. Although he had dropped in the rankings from 20 to 63 over two years, I was positive this was not due to his lack of ability with a tennis racquet or athleticism, it was what I called his 'warrior mentality', that ball of fire deep down in his belly which relished the battle and acted on instinct alone.

At two sets down, I figured I had to shock him into action with a lot of bad language and yelling about the three more hours we had to go, the 'war of attrition' we were to begin, the ball of fire deep down in his belly he had to rediscover if he was to win the war of attrition, and how at the end of this we were going to bury his opponent so far under the court they would never find him.

Shock stuff, but it worked, and Pat's career was reborn, as he went on to become number one in the world. As he got rid of all the outside noise, he allowed his mind and body to do their job.

With Lleyton, he had always been confident and proud of his mental and physical ability to stay the course. A strange virus that had been with him for four months had put doubt into his mind about how long he could last, knowing full well it would take him about four hours for victory.

I was pretty sure he would begin having some serious self-doubt around the two-hour mark and I had a plan, but all I said to him pre-match was that as soon as he felt his body was in trouble he had to let me know because I had a way to help him. It was a gamble, but I knew Lleyton pretty well and felt confident that he had trust in me.

Again it was the subconscious mind telling Lleyton he had been having trouble for four months and therefore victory was beyond him. We shut out all that negative noise and concentrated solely on restoring energy to the body by deep breathing and blowing out all the negative rubbish that had accumulated. Once Lleyton believed this, his mind became quiet and his physical ability returned.

At age 58, I had a personal experience that really tested my ability to maintain a quiet mind. I was attending a corporate function in Brisbane and had just finished a speech when I felt something like a small electric shock go through my head followed by a feeling of slight dizziness. Not sure of what had happened, I went back to my hotel and woke at 6 a.m. for an 8 a.m. flight back home to Sydney.

As I got ready to shave, I wondered what the episode was the previous night. The answer came pretty quickly as I discovered my right hand was having trouble directing the razor. A further disturbing clue as I checked out was when I realised my speech was slurred.

As I sat in the back of the hire car on the way to the airport, I faced the fact that I'd probably had some kind of stroke and needed to make a decision – go to an emergency ward or fly back to Sydney where I knew top medical people and could get the best of attention. The downside of my going to a Brisbane hospital was they would certainly not allow me to fly home. The downside of flying was another brain attack at 10,000 metres.

I decided on flying but made a firm decision that I needed to put myself in a zone where I thought of nothing, a kind of meditation, in other words a 100 per cent quiet mind which would help keep my body relaxed.

By 11 a.m. I was checking into a private hospital in Sydney and found I had lost most use of my right hand, as I could not write or print my name on checking in. The next couple of days were full of pressure as the doctors did all sorts of tests to make sure there were no blood clots floating around that could create some very serious problems.

I was lucky, as the small blood vessel that burst had sealed off. If it had kept bleeding things would have developed badly. My writing hand returned after four months, I had some numbness in the right of my bottom lip for 12 months and some small issues with the right foot.

Doctors said that it was probably the wrong move to get on the plane and no doubt they were right. I believe my decision to maintain a 'quiet mind' played an important role in no further damage occurring.

Mike's response

There are many challenges in today's more complex world and I believe that what enables a small minority to really succeed in these more challenging times is that they are focused and more present to their situation. I see people with targets to achieve each month who find their mindspace occupied with so many thoughts and so much activity distracting them from their most pressing challenge – making their numbers. Their fears, negative thoughts, contemplation of so many hypotheticals, mean that their mindspace is not focused on the job at hand, their mind is cluttered.

It all starts with your view of yourself. If you can reconnect with the fact that you are enough and let go of your insecurities and doubts, then your mindspace will become a lot quieter as your subconscious mind checks out. Quietening down the Negative Force, as Newk describes it.

Imagine how much more effective and successful you could be if the tasks that you undertook each day had your full and undivided attention, if you stayed completely focused on the outcomes you wanted to achieve with a clear and effective mind, with good thought processes and congruency in each element of the MINDsense model.

Chapter 11

Peak Performance

Newk

> If you can force your heart and nerve and sinew
> To serve your turn long after they are gone,
> And so hold on when there is nothing in you
> Except the Will which says to them: 'Hold on!'

I have over time been fascinated by human endeavour and stories about men and women who have been able to operate efficiently long after they believed their resources were exhausted. I had always prepared myself physically and mentally for Grand Slam tournaments where four-hour singles matches might occur, and in my time the top players also played doubles.

So it was that, until nearing the end of my career, although I had been really tested several times, I had never gone into that place or that period of time where you are performing at a very high level but actually have no real sense or memory of what is happening. For the sake of a better terminology, I call it the time I had an inner body experience and after that Kipling's words had new meaning for me.

By mid-1973 we were about to have our third child and I was seriously considering retirement. I was 29 years old, had achieved more than my dreams, and travel connected to time away from home and my family was making me an unhappy camper.

Although I had won the Australian Open in January and helped the Davis Cup team reach the semi-finals, we hadn't played at Wimbledon due to a players' boycott, and I had hardly played any tournaments. My world ranking had slipped to ten and I suppose people were starting to think of me as yesterday's champion.

In mid-July I told my wife Angie of my decision to retire and her only comment was, 'Are you sure? I think you should seriously consider this for a couple of days!'

As I had learnt that most smart men listen closely to the advice of a good wife, I took a couple of days and realised I would be quitting at a time when my mental and physical strength was still very strong, even though I had actually slipped off the radar as one of the world's leading players. Was that how I wanted to depart a journey that had begun 20 years earlier? My answer was no!

So I said to Angie I'd decided to play for nine months and give it everything I had. My aim was to win the US Open in four weeks' time, the Davis Cup in December, and the WCT finals in Dallas the following May. To do this, I said I would have to be single-minded and selfish towards the family, so if she preferred I didn't take on the challenge I would not do it.

I got an affirmative and supportive answer from Angie and proceeded to go to work on myself and my game for the four weeks leading into the US Open. Over the next nine months, I achieved my three goals and by May 1974 I was number one in the world.

What I hadn't thought through was, 'What do I do now?' I played the 1974 Wimbledon championship and then the US Open, losing in the quarters and semis respectively, while the hottest new boy Jimmy Connors, whom I had beaten in the 1973 US Open quarters, won both of those Slams. By the end of 1974, he was number one and I was number two. This in itself was not an issue for me; it was more that we had not played each other since my win in the 1973 US Open.

By mid-November, the season was at an end and I let the Australian Open organisers know that I would be retiring and not competing in that Grand Slam, which was to begin in four weeks' time.

Ten days before the start of that event, I got a phone call to say Connors was definitely coming and would I change my mind? Without hesitation, I said if you guarantee it, then you can put me in the draw.

I hadn't played for four weeks and had not been doing any physical training, so I had ten days to get my body into some sort of shape. I set out a five-kilometre run around our suburban streets which had a one-kilometre section up a very steep hill.

I named this 'Connors Hill' and when I was feeling tired about two-thirds of the way up I would imagine I was 5–5 in the fifth set with Connors and my body was starting to give in on me. Every day I sprinted the last third of the hill and would proceed to do a 'Rocky'-like jog at the top. It is a pretty busy road, so I can only imagine what the drivers and passengers were thinking as they went by.

The daily run was around noon, which was nice and hot during Sydney's summer. Normally I would have practised on the court for three or four hours a day, but due to the lack of time I felt my physical body needed the work if I were to survive seven five-set matches plus the doubles, as my body was going to be tested to its limits. Little did I know how true this was.

My tennis game, as expected, was rusty and the first-round encounter, against a German I would normally beat in three sets, took five sets and three hours. The good news was that my body responded well during and after the match.

As the two-week event went on, the weather became a serious problem, so much so that the final was due to be played on Wednesday, January 1st, and we were playing our quarter-final singles and doubles on Monday, December 30th. My form was still scratchy and I just managed to beat Geoff Masters 10–8 in the fifth set in a match lasting almost four hours. This was followed by doubles quarters with Tony Roche and me moving through to the next day's semis.

My semi-final was to be against Tony and these were always tough, gruelling encounters. I spent two hours the night before that match with our Davis Cup trainer, Stan Nicholles, who worked hard to push all the build-up of lactic acid out of my legs. Meanwhile, on the other side of the draw, Connors was advancing without too much trouble. Now that I had made the semis, my mindset was 100 per cent on reaching the final for a showdown that the media had been building up since the two of us had decided to play.

My semi-final with Tony was a gruelling match and I finally beat him 11–9 in the fifth set. The match took over four hours, but it was during the last 45 minutes that I went into a place inside my body and mind that

I had never been before. Tony led 5–2 in that final set and had four match points before I finally won.

My memory of such classical encounters is usually quite vivid, but in this case I had no memory from 5–2 for the rest of the set. After the match the on-court interviewer Mike Williamson walked over to my chair where I was sitting with a towel over my head. Mike told me two days later: 'I asked you to do an interview on court and you looked up at me from under the towel. I had done quite a few boxing fights in my time and I could see in your eyes that faraway look that said you had been somewhere deep inside your body, an experience not too many people have during their lives! I realised you were probably not able to talk without breaking down, so I left you there.'

My only memory was sitting in the chair with the towel over my head and having a great desire to break down and cry.

I had to default the doubles semis and again spent two hours with Stan working on my legs. The next day, Connors and I had a classic encounter which I managed to win 7–6 in the fourth set. I served for it at 5–3, Connors broke back and then held a set point to take it into a fifth set when he served at 6–5 in the tiebreak. Had we gone into a fifth set, I had no idea how I was going to respond physically, as I felt I had been working on reserve fuel for some time.

When these things are happening, you tend not to think about them too much at the time; however, when I thought the final days through a couple of days later, I realised that I had experienced something very special.

What is the human spirit and how far can it be

pushed? The way I read the last 45 minutes of the semi-final I had pushed myself into a space inside my body where time was irrelevant and the only thing of importance was to achieve the goal of reaching the final with Connors; after that the best man would win on the day.

So where exactly was I, in some deep part of my mind and brain, or had I gone into the deeper part of my inner soul which had been developed through 14 years of tough experience on the battlefield of world tennis? What I do know is I had no recollection of that last 45 minutes, something I had never before experienced.

The reason I commenced this story 18 months prior to the Australian Open is because happenings like this do not simply occur; it is the build-up over a period of time that creates the atmosphere. My decision to continue playing in pursuit of excellence in July 1973 and the ongoing series of events I am sure led to my deep emotional state. For example, one wonders what would have happened had I not won the US Open six weeks after I declared my crusade!

I now keenly await Mike's take on what I have laid out. I have never discussed this issue with him before, so I am interested to see how he answers the challenge!

Mike's response

Wow, I must say it feels like Newk has just fired down one of his famous big first serves and I've got to find a way somehow to return it!

To explore Newk's experience and understand

where he was during that 45-minute period late in the fifth set, we first need to understand thought processes and how the memory of an event is created. This may sound a little complicated but I'm sure you will quickly see its relevance, particularly as it can help to guide us to the place from which peak performance can flow.

The mind is the source from which all perception, intuition and movement originate. Our mental state is even responsible for why and how we engage in action in the first place. The state of our mind is the key to everything.

While reflecting on Newk's experience of that 45-minute period of the match, it occurred to me that his experience had a lot of similarities with the state people achieve when they are meditating. At this point you may be wondering what a sporting battle has to do with the more spiritual world of meditation and the answer is that they both rely to such a large extent on our state of mind and our ability to harness the power of the mind.

Like most people, I used to think that peak or extreme performance levels were more likely to occur when we were thinking well with great focus; however over the years I have found that peak performance is more likely to flow when we silence the mind, when the subconscious mind is quiet. This state is often referred to as being 'in the zone'.

To help explain this, I need to go back to my earlier Zen study and the teachings of my Zen master, Roshi Kitabu Turner. Zen explores the nature of the mind and has great relevance to extreme performance.

In Zen teachings there is a focus on thought-

179

impulses, or, as they are called in Japanese, '*nen*'. In particular, Zen focuses on differentiating between these thought processes. According to these teachings, the mind operates in a particular way, processing 'only one *nen* at a time'. You cannot really do two things at once because you cannot be conscious of two things at once.

The first thought impulse or *nen* action takes place before we are actually aware of it. The mind is processing the 'event' before we have actually processed the awareness of the 'event'. Then the second thought impulse is the awareness of the first impulse. That is, it takes a separate *nen* action to become aware of the first *nen* action – a reflection on the first thought process. This reflection is the second *nen*.

There is a strong connection between the martial arts and Zen. As far back as the thirteenth century, Zen and martial traditions began influencing each other. Zen explores the nature of the mind and centuries ago it was realised that our ability to survive combat was not so much about the speed of our sword but the speed and power of our mind.

As I have stated earlier, what separates the great achievers from the rest is strength of mind. There is no doubt that Newk had a great tennis game and wonderful athleticism, but I have always believed, as I have observed him in all facets of life, that his strength of mind and within that, his self-belief was his greatest asset. It enabled him to take his finely honed skills and achieve world number one status.

Perhaps Newk was operating in a Zen-like state without actually being aware of it as such.

The first *nen* is associated with the initial experience of something and is accompanied by an unconscious response or action. For example, if a truck crosses to your side of the road and you are in immediate danger there is the initial thought impulse that recognises the situation before you are conscious of it, followed often by a spontaneous action to avoid the truck. What follows then is the second *nen* or the reflection on and awareness of your situation. You realise what has happened.

There are several factors that influence how spontaneous our reaction is to a situation and therefore our effectiveness in responding to it. The first is our awareness of our environment and how tuned in we are to it – the consciousness we have of our surroundings. This aids in our ability almost to see something before it happens. The acuteness of our awareness allows the mind to project forward events that are unfolding before us.

The second factor is the availability of our mindspace. Previously we have discussed the notion that we have one mindspace but two 'minds' that are competing for the resources of that mindspace. The subconscious mind brings with it all the self-validating noise associated with the past and the conscious mind processes our instructions. For most human beings, the subconscious mind dominates and we experience different levels of background 'noise' depending on how much we subconsciously need to validate that we are 'enough'.

Our response time to a situation, the speed of our spontaneity, is also influenced by how much 'noise' is occupying the mindspace and diminishing our awareness of our situation. 'I didn't see it coming' is often the response of someone whose mindspace is so occupied with subconscious noise that there is limited mental capacity available for awareness.

This may sound as if I am suggesting that we have to wander around in a heightened state of consciousness, acutely aware of everything that is going on around us. If you are in a war zone where your life is constantly under threat, or alone in a jungle that is home to dangerous beasts, this state of consciousness will come in very useful. It will require great concentration, however, and after a period of time mental fatigue will occur and your consciousness will drop. This will be when you are most vulnerable.

Fortunately, most of us don't live in circumstances where our lives are constantly under threat. For us this level of constant situational awareness and consciousness is not required. Perhaps if we learnt to operate in an increased level of consciousness, though, we might find that our ability to deal with our daily circumstances improved. We would find ourselves 'ahead of the game' and operating and responding with greater speed.

The alternative to this state of constant consciousness is to find the state of no mind, known in Zen as *mushin*. My translation of this is the state where the mindspace is not occupied by either the conscious or subconscious mind. The mindspace is empty. If you have ever experienced a car trip where you have arrived at your destination and then suddenly become aware (conscious) that you have no recollection of the journey, then you have experienced the state of no mind.

This is more about the lack of subconscious noise

than anything else. The need for self-validation does not exist at this time so the subconscious mind has no role to play and sits quietly on the sidelines. The mind-space is now empty and quiet, ready and waiting to offer all of its resources to our thought impulses and then the conscious mind as we engage it – that is, a mind not occupied by thought or emotion and thus available completely. It is sometimes described as 'being in flow', a state experienced by artists in a creative process and sports people in the moment of elite performance.

I got a good understanding of the concept from watching the movie *The Matrix* and in particular the fight training scene between Neo and Morpheus. Morpheus was teaching Neo to get his mind out of the way. As he says in the scene, stop thinking, it's slowing you down.

Mushin, or the state of no mind, is achieved when a person's mind is free from thoughts. There is an absence of distracting thoughts and judgement, so the person is totally free to act and react towards a situation without hesitation and without distraction from such thoughts. At this point, a person relies not on what they think should be the next move, but what is their trained reaction or what is felt intuitively. It is not a state of relaxed near-sleep, however. The mind is probably working at a very high speed, but with no distractions, just great clarity about the moment they are experiencing.

In Zen the analogy often used is to compare a clear mind to a still pond. The still pond is able to clearly reflect the moon and trees, but just as ripples across the surface of the pond will distort the picture of reality, so will the thoughts we hold on to disrupt the flow of our instinctive and highly trained actions.

On the negative side, the process of 'choking' in sport occurs when the mind gets in the way. We witness highly trained athletes who have put many hours into their sport and who have executed the shot or the kick or the jump many times before, only this time they cannot clear their mind of the noise of negativity. This distracting noise disrupts the flow of action.

In meditation we learn to empty the mind of thoughts and to just 'be', to exist in stillness in the moment. In terms of thought impulses, meditation is about staying in the first *nen*, completely present to our situation without reflecting on our situation.

In normal thought, the first and second *nen* come and go momentarily, and the pattern repeats at speed as the process of thought takes place. The first and second *nen* will intermix and appear as one.

The second thought impulse, or second *nen*, is the thought process that recognises the first thought impulse or the first *nen*. The second *nen* allows us to analyse and evaluate the first *nen*. It is our awareness of our situation and the reflection on it. Although we can think of these as being two separate operations, they appear to us as one.

It would seem that the second thought impulse, the awareness of the situation, is the process that commits the situation to memory. Our recognition of the situation commits it to memory. If there is no awareness or second *nen*, then no memory of the situation is created.

I am not sure how Newk came to find himself in this space, but it would seem pretty clear that he was operating without reflection, completely present to his circumstances and with a mind completely available to deal with his circumstances. Perhaps it was exhaustion and what little energy his mind and body had was being preserved for playing tennis. I tend to think, though, that it was probably achieved through extraordinary focus.

Remember, this was the culmination of a prolonged focus on achieving an outcome. From the moment Newk got the phone call telling him that Connors had entered the Australian Open to this point in time, it was all about the opportunity to challenge Jimmy Connors. Now it was within grasp and all those five-set matches along the way had to be for something.

At 5–2 down in the fifth set and with his dream slipping away, Newk found himself very focused and present to his circumstances. As the intensity of his focus kicked in, all thought now had to be on each point. It was no good concerning himself with the outcome of the match; that was almost gone. He had to dig incredibly deep and inch by inch crawl out of the hole he was in.

This level of intense focus is often evident before elite performers enter the zone. It brings everything down to the moment and how to deal with that moment. When the moment is dealt with, there is no reflection. There is no time to reflect; they need to be ready for the next moment. Their mind is not concerned with the future and nor is it caught up in the past, it is very present. This is 'the zone'. This is where elite performance takes place.

Elite performers would have to train for many years to be capable of maintaining this state of *mushin* or no mind. Over this time their techniques are practised many thousands of times, until they can be performed spontaneously, without conscious thought, thus allowing their reactions to be more effective in whatever they may be doing. It is not necessarily an easy state to reach, nor had Newk been practising to be able to attain it, which probably explains why he only experienced it very rarely.

As each point was played, Newk would experience his first thought impulse as the ball was hit by Tony Roche. Such was his awareness of the situation, so present was he to the moment, that he could tune in with great accuracy to Tony's racquet head and the sound of the ball off the strings. This gave him a 'head start' in his preparation and Tony probably started to feel that Newk was able to read his mind.

The first *nen* or thought impulse is accompanied by spontaneous action and, given the thousands of hours of practice and the thousands of matches Newk had played, his techniques and reactions had been incredibly well drilled. He was able to execute without distraction, without the thoughts of outcomes, without any mind noise at all. It became a performance in the state of flow.

Newk's response

I was really interested to see how Mike responded to the challenge. I knew I had been in some kind of mindspace where everything happened correctly, but I have never been sure of how to explain it.

Well done, Mike. In my opinion you have nailed it.

Newk's Eight Key Messages for Life

Positive Energy vs Negative Energy

In life there is both Positive Energy and Negative Energy. One can be your best friend, the other your worst enemy. Learn to process them consciously to your benefit.

Dealing with Triumph and Disaster

As Kipling says, they are impostors. Don't get so caught up with success that you get a big head and don't get too hard and down on yourself if you don't succeed. Learn that life is a journey between these two extremes and the middle of the road is a lot more friendly if you can live with these extremes.

Never Be Afraid to Dream

It's great to dream but dreams on their own are cheap. Follow your dream. Give yourself the chance to experience your dreams by doing what you need to do and learning to believe what you need to believe. You can achieve great things if you try and keep trying. Don't make your dream your master, though. Allow the road to change, just keep moving forward.

He Who Aims High Never Falls Low

If you aim for the stars and the moon and fall short, you'll probably find yourself at the top of the mountain. If you aim for the top of the mountain and fall short, you'll find yourself half way up; and if you aim for the foot of the mountain and fall short you won't get very far at all.

If the Deal Is Too Good to Be True – the Deal Is Too Good to Be True

Adhering to this will save you a lot of anxiety, stress, time and money. Why do we get drawn into these kinds of deals? Because we allow hope to sway our common sense and our desire for success to validate that we are enough distorts our thinking. We consciously know that it can't be that good, but our subconscious mind is running the show and it wants validation and the spoils of success. Hope distracts us.

Follow First Your Heart, Then Your Head and Finally Your Gut Instinct

I believe that from our heart flow our purest desires, those that connect with our highest purpose in life. We might also call this our calling in life. When you have identified this, engage your mind – your conscious mind – to process your approach. Use the MINDsense model. Finally, trust your gut instinct. It is your mind processing at 'warp speed' all of the information relative to the journey. How often is it wrong? Learn to trust it.

Think About and Acknowledge the Past, Contemplate the Future, but Always Live in the Present

The past is where we learn our lessons from our past experiences. Go there to learn, not to be right about what was right or wrong with what has been. See the future with belief and let go of the self-doubt. Be present to the moment you are in right now. If every moment in your life gets the best version of you, focused and present with a quiet mind, imagine what your life will be.

Practise Your Listening Skills – Speech Is Silver, Silence Is Golden

I never met a person who was able to learn anything while they were talking. God gave us two ears and one mouth so that we could listen twice as much as we speak.

Mike's Eight Key Messages for Life

Wake Up. It's Time to Take Control of Your Mind

Consciousness is the key. Without it you are not in control. Your subconscious mind's agenda is about preservation and validation. That doesn't support growth and change. Learn to engage your conscious mind and think your way to success.

Learn to Understand the Connection Between Beliefs, Emotions, Behaviours and Results

Understand the MINDsense model and if your beliefs, emotions and actions are congruent with your desired result, it will happen.

Own Your Life and Be Who You Choose to Be

Consciously connect with the experiences that created your current sense of yourself and let them go. Now make a choice. Define yourself, be who you want to be.

Take Responsibility for Your Emotions

Stop blaming others or events for how you feel. Your emotions take place inside your physiology. They are a consequence of your reaction to your circumstances. Without consciousness your subconscious will use your circumstances to validate that you are enough by being right about them. With consciousness you have a choice. Make that choice and own how you feel. Now you can take the most appropriate action more often and with less wasted time.

If You Don't Believe in it, it Won't Happen!

Our actions, thoughts and ability to make something happen are underpinned by our beliefs. If you don't believe, you won't take the necessary actions and your thoughts won't support your desired outcomes.

A Quiet, Focused Mind Gets the Job Done

Clear the distractions of your subconscious mind by taking it out of play by reconnecting with being enough again, just as you were when you were born. There is often a lot to contemplate as we take on life's challenges. Don't make it any harder by only bringing a small portion of your mindspace to the task. Bring all of your mind and see how much more effective you become.

Never Lower Your Standards

You know what you want, have the courage to go after it!

Growth and moving forward in life are a consequence of goals and aspirations. The gap between where I am now and where I want to be is where dissatisfaction 'lives'. Use that dissatisfaction to drive action – action supported by the belief that you can.

Think About How You Think

Take the time to analyse how well you are thinking and be prepared to make changes. Practise the process of thinking that the MINDsense model delivers.

About the Authors

John Newcombe

John Newcombe is a tennis legend. During his career he won 26 Grand Slam Titles including three Wimbledons, two US Opens and two Australian singles titles. He also led Australia to the title in 1999 as Davis Cup Captain. He has been inducted into the International Tennis Hall of Fame and was made an Australian Living Treasure.

In addition to a commentating career, he now runs the John Newcombe Tennis Ranch & Tennis Academy in New Braunfels, Texas. Established in 1968, the ranch is one of the premier tennis destinations in the world, offering a world class tennis academy and fantasy camps with tennis legends.

Michael Duff

Michael Duff is one of Australia's leading coaches of High Performance Human Behaviour, with a client list that reads like a who's who of the country's leading companies. He has spent his career in the corporate sector leading teams and organisations very similar to those he now teaches.

At age 28 Michael was appointed Chief Executive of the Australasian PGA tour and from here joined the global ATP tour where he spent five years in contact with the world's top tennis players. He spent a decade as a senior executive in the international sporting world and he continues to seek out high achievers from all walks of life.

Acknowledgements

First and foremost I must thank Newk for the opportunity to work with him on this book. Over the 20 years we have been friends, his counsel, support and guidance has been one of the great blessings of my life and a wonderful inspiration.

To my late mum Jill, who taught me the power of consciousness from a very early age with her constant encouragement to 'think about what you are going to do or say first'. Her continual expressions of belief in me and my ability was the greatest gift any mother can give her child.

To my dad John, the opportunity to acknowledge what you have done for me is one I cherish. As a role model for me as I entered adulthood and as a great friend throughout my life I have always been grateful for your strong, calm presence in my life. I do not know of anyone who has lived their life with more integrity than you.

My gorgeous daughters Alexandra and Lucy (Secret Squirrel and Little Chicken). You are the sunshine in my life. I am so very proud of both of you and of the beautiful women you have become. Nothing makes me prouder than watching you both grow in life.

To the extraordinary woman behind the scenes who has allowed me to lead the wonderful life that I have, my darling wife Eleanor. She is the major part of the team, the one who has selflessly supported my journey and been there at every turn. Without you, none of this would have been possible.

To Terry, Lois, Kathy, Tony, Gary, Sandra, Roy, Gretel, Tom, Chris, David, Chrisso, Johnno, Megs, Steph, Emma and Nicki, your presence in my life contributes so much fun and joy. And to my two old mates Boyd White and Stephen Scherer who have been in 'my corner' forever. I love you all and am blessed.

And finally, to my other two champion mates, Guy Leech and Anh Do. Thank you Leechy for teaching me the power of a strong, clear sense of self. It's little wonder that you are the great success that you are and a top bloke as well. To Anh for his never-ending enthusiasm for life, his great passion for all that he does and that incredible smile that is surely one of our national treasures. Your friendship means so much to me.